The Ramadan Discourses
of Shaykh Muhammad ibn al-Habib

The Ramadan Discourses

of

Shaykh Muhammad ibn al-Habib

1288/1871 – 1391/1972

Translated by:
Abdalhaqq Bewley, Safwan Najjar,
and Abdalqadir al-Harkassi

The Ramadan Discourses of Shaykh Muhammad ibn al-Habib

Published by: Diwan Press Ltd.
311 Allerton Road
Bradford
BD15 7HA
UK
Website: www.diwanpress.com
E-mail: info@diwanpress.com

Author: Shaykh Muhammad ibn al-Habib
Translated by: Abdalhaqq Bewley, Safwan Najjar, and Abdalqadir al-Harkassi
Edited by: Abdalhaqq Bewley

A catalogue record of this book is available from the British Library.

ISBN-13:   978-1-914397-28-8 (casebound)
                978-1-914397-29-5 (paperback)
                978-1-914397-30-1 (ePub and Kindle)

Cover photo by kind permission of Peter Sanders

Contents

بسم الله الرحمن الرحيم
وصلى الله على سيدنا و مولانا محمد
و اله و صحبه اجمعين و سلم تسليما

Preface

The *tafsir* discourses in this book were recorded during Ramadan in October 1971 just two months before Shaykh Muhammad ibn al-Habib died in Algeria on his way to Hajj. They are the only recordings ever made of the teaching of the Shaykh and, as such, represent an extremely precious element of his legacy. His teaching discourses almost always took the form of giving a *tafsir* of Quranic *ayahs* that had just been recited and these discourses follow that pattern. It was his custom in Ramadan year on year to remain in Meknes during the entire month and go through the Qur'an from end to end, starting in one Ramadan where he had finished the previous year. In this, his last Ramadan, he began half way through *ayah* 156 of *Sura al-A'raf,* which was where he had reached the year before.

It must be remembered, as can be seen from the short biography that introduces this volume, that Shaykh Muhammad ibn al-Habib completed his studies at the very beginning of the 20th Century, certainly before 1905. This means that he was from the last generation of scholars whose entire education took place before the intervention of any colonial administration into the Moroccan education system. So he was the direct legatee of a traditional education process that had been continuing unbroken in Fez for more than a millennium and that was completely unaffected by the ethos of scientific materialism which the colonial powers brought in their wake and which now dominates the entire world.

This is clearly reflected in his teaching which comes across with a freshness and authenticity and freedom from any modernist influence that no scholar of subsequent generations has been genuinely able to achieve.

This is reflected in everything he says but is demonstrated particularly clearly in his continual insistence on a pure understanding of *tawhid*. This is something he emphasised generally throughout his teaching and, as can be seen, he returns to it again and again in these discourses. Something else that shines through in his words is his constant, almost urgent, awareness of the Divine Presence and the reality of the Next World, and his fervent desire to communicate that to his hearers so that they realise the true nature of the human situation and their need to act upon what he says. This has made these discourses as relevant, or even more relevant, than they were when they were first delivered fifty years ago.

The doctrines of scientific materialism, positing, as they do, the absolute reality of cause and effect, have now penetrated even more deeply into human consciousness and have made it vital that the true teaching of *tawhid* is once more made accessible to Muslims in the way it is through the Shaykh's words here. And the rampant secularism that now dominates virtually the whole world, which treats the Divine Presence and the realities of the Next World at best as myth and frequently as fiction, makes the Shaykh's certainty about them and vibrant awareness of them all the more inspiring and needed in the present time. May Allah greatly benefit all who read these discourses and increase the reward of Shaykh Muhammad ibn al-Habib by the benefit they bring.

Abdalhaqq Bewley

A brief summary of the life of Shaykh Sidi Muhammad ibn al-Habib, may Allah purify his secret, by Bashir ibn Isma'il

Praise be to Allah, the Generous Bestowing Helper, and blessings and peace be upon our Master Muhammad, the adornment of existence and glory of the worlds, and upon his pure good family and glorious Companions, and may He be pleased with those who love them and follow them, and those who follow them and who follow in their footsteps in the best way until the Day of Rising.

This is a brief biography written to act as a treasure trove for lovers to help them learn about the life of someone by whose clear light souls have been illuminated and by whose clear secret hearts have been guided: the spiritual Qutb and luminous Muhammadan man, our teacher, model and fount of our blessing, Sidi Muhammad ibn al-Habib al-Amghari al-Idrisi al-Hasani. May Allah purify his secret and soul and let us benefit from his *baraka*!

It is not concealed from any intelligent person that the biography of this gnostic of Allah – and that of those *awliya'* of Allah like him – is not just a matter of telling a life story or transmitting information. Such biographies are rather salutary reminders and extremely beneficial narratives, testifying to pure souls who have come into this world to transmit to other people a noble message they have been trusted to pass on. They perform that task fully and comprehensively and then travel on to a more resplendent World, leaving behind them a straight path, pure character and

1

an excellent example. Those who write the lives of the righteous agree that the writing of the biographies of the *awliya'* of Allah constitutes one of the greatest means of drawing near to Allah since the *rahamut* (intense divine mercy) descends when they are mentioned and great blessings follow one after another. And they also agree that reading about their lives engenders feelings of love for them in the heart, strengthens the yearning to be close to them and spurs people on to model themselves on them.

As we write this much needed biography of our shaykh, Sidi Muhammad ibn al-Habib ﷺ, we can only ask Allah, the Gracious and Ever-Giving, that people will take benefit from it and that those who read it or hear it will spread it, reflect on it and, indeed, will correct any unintended mistakes it may contain. We ask Allah, the Almighty and Majestic, to make it a rich source of nourishment, a treasure trove and a fount of knowledge which will encourage everyone who reads it to show proper respect towards this righteous *wali*, to love him with deep abiding love, and that it may fill them with yearning to be near him and join him. Amen. Amen. Amen. Praise be to Allah, the Lord of the worlds.

His origins and youth

He is the deeply learned, consummate scholar with profound understanding, the Shaykh of the *Tariqa*, the connecting link joining the *Shari'a* and the *Haqiqa*, the unique Muhammadan individual, the teacher of hearts and souls, the guide to the path of true happiness and success, Shaykh Sidi Muhammad ibn al-Habib ibn as-Siddiq al-Amghari al-Idrisi al-Hasani al-Fasi (of Fes by birth and youth), al-Maknasi (of Meknes by residence and final resting-place), al-Maliki by *madhhab*, ash-Shadhili by *tariqa*. He

🌺 was descended from the righteous *wali*, Moulay Abu ʿAbdullah, Sidi Muhammad ibn ʿAbdullah, the Hasani Idrisi sharif known as Amghar, from the Amghari sayyids, the people of ʿAyn al-Fitr called Titanfitr which is now known as Tit.[i] The Amghari sayyids are Idrisid sharifs descended from Moulay ʿAbdullah ibn Moulay Idris 🌺. Amghar is a Berber word meaning "shaykh". It was the title of their grandfather, the perfect Qutb and gnostic of Allah, the realised, the famous shaykh and support, Abu ʿAbdullah Sidi Muhammad Amghar who is buried at Azammur, and known as the great and greatest Amghar.

The family of the Amghari sharifs is a blessed family of noble prominent scholars and imams who had a considerable role in spreading knowledge and righteousness in Morocco. Ibn Qunfudh al-Qusantini said, speaking of them in his book *Uns al-Faqir*: 'This household is the greatest household in Morocco with regard to righteousness because they passed it on as a legacy, generation after generation, as people pass on wealth.'[1] One of the ancestors of Sidi Muhammad ibn al-Habib moved to Tafilalet, more specifically to the Qasr of the sons of Sidi Yusuf at ar-Rissani, and settled there. Then his father, Sidi al-Habib ibn as-Siddiq emigrated from there to Fes and took up residence there.

According to the soundest position, our beloved shaykh 🌺 was born into this good, noble, and blessed family in 1288/1871. He grew up as a young man of noble character and pleasing

---

i   Tit is located on the Atlantic coast in the district of Dukala, about 11 km from El-Jadida. Today it is known as the centre of Moulay ʿAbdullah. It is considered to be one of the ancient inhabited centres of Morocco.

qualities under the protection of his parents, surrounded by their tenderness and care as he was their only child.

His memorisation of the Noble Qur'an

In his childhood in the year 1293/1876 he entered the *mahdara* (Qur'an school) at the Abu'r-Ru'us Bridge in the Sharabiliyyin quarter of Fes where, in a short period, he memorised a considerable portion of the Noble Qur'an from the *faqih* and righteous *wali*, Sidi Ibn al-Hashimi as-Sanhaji ﷺ. He continued his memorisation under the *faqih* Sidi Ahmad al-Filali ﷺ in the *mahdara* (Qur'an school) of Qasba an-Nawwar. It is related that one of the *awliya'* of Allah Almighty visited that Qur'an school, spoke with the *faqih*, Ahmad al-Filali, and then examined the students with an eye of deep discernment (*firasa*), illuminated by inspiration from Allah Almighty about what they would become. He pointed at each of them in turn, saying, 'This one will be a butcher. This one will be a tailor,' and so forth, and indeed, in the fullness of time, each of those students became what was disclosed about them. When he reached our Shaykh ﷺ, he said about him, 'This one will be a scholar who acts on his knowledge, someone scrupulous who remembers Allah, a teaching shaykh.' And the perspicacity of that *wali* proved to be true. Praise be Allah!

His shaykhs in the memorisation of the Noble Qur'an also included Sidi Muhammad ibn al-Hasan, one of the descendants of the righteous *wali* of lofty station, Sidi 'Abd as-Salam ibn Mashish ﷺ. Our shaykh used to assist him in his trade of tailoring, tying the warp for him, and when he finished doing that, he would busy himself with his tablet and memorise what he had written on it. It is said that our shaykh's father, Sidi al-Habib ﷺ, learned of this and was angry about it. He went to Sidi Muhammad ibn al-Hasan to complain to him about that, thinking that his son was being distracted by that work from learning the Qur'an. Sidi Muhammad ibn al-Hasan received him, however, with friendliness, kindness and esteem, and gave him the good news that his son Muhammad would, by Allah's permission, memorise the Noble Qur'an very quickly and would, if Allah willed, become a man of great importance and that great men and outstanding scholars would be trained by him.

As soon as this excellent father heard these good tidings his alarm was dispelled and his heart set at rest. He left, praising Allah Almighty for the blessing of this righteous son. Two years passed and Sidi Muhammad ibn al-Habib memorised the Noble Qur'an for the third time and began to assist his shaykh in teaching other children. After that, as was the custom, his shaykh asked him to memorise the basic texts and read the fundamental books and so he devoted himself to texts of *fiqh*, grammar and language, both in terms of memorisation and understanding, until he had completed what was necessary in that respect and done so comprehensively. When he had accomplished that his shaykh summoned him and said to him, 'May Allah bless you, my son. You have achieved what I desired you to achieve. Now my task with you is complete, so go to the Qarawiyyin mosque to complete your studies. May Allah help you.'

His quest for knowledge at the Qarawiyyin Mosque

Our shaykh – may Allah purify his secret – went to the Qarawiyyin mosque and began to take from the oceans of knowledge there and constantly kept company with esteemed shaykhs who were known for realisation, precision and righteousness. He ﷺ related about those shaykhs, 'I used to study the areas of outward knowledge with the Shaykh of the Community and Shaykh al-Islam, Ahmad ibn al-Khayyat, with the accomplished scholar, Sidi Abu Bakr Bannani, with the *faqih* 'Abd as-Salam al-Huwari, with the head of the Majlis al-'Ilmi as-Sufi, the accomplished Sidi Ahmad ibn al-Jaylali, with the *sharif* and blessing, Sidi Muhammad al-Qadiri, with the eloquent scholar, Sidi Khalil at-Tilimsani, with the *sharif* and blessing, Sidi Muhammad ibn Ja'far al-Kittani, with Sidi at-Tuhami Kannun, and with the leader of the *sharifs*, the *hafiz* who was accomplished in many types of knowledge, particularly knowledge of *hadith*, Moulay 'Abdullah al-Badrawi, and the one eager to benefit his students, the author Sidi Muhammad al-Irari.'

The details of his scholarly life are too long to go into in full, but there is no harm in indicating some of those under whom he studied. Among them were:

- Sidi Shaykh Muhammad al-Irari ﷺ with whom he studied the rules of *tajwid* and *al-Ajrumiyya*;
- Sidi Shaykh Ahmad ibn al-Jaylali al-Amghari ﷺ, the head of the Majlis al-'Ilmi as-Sufi, with whom he studied the *Mukhtasar* of Shaykh Khalil with [the commentaries of] az-Zurqani, Banani and al-Kharshi;
- Sidi Shaykh at-Tawdi ibn Sawda ﷺ with whom he studied *Tuhfa al-Ahwadhi*, a commentary on the *Sunan* of at-Tirmidhi;
- Sidi Shaykh Abu Bakr ibn al-'Arabi with whom he studied the *Collection of the Adab of the Teacher and the Student* by Shaykh Khalil;

- Sidi Shaykh Ahmad ibn al-Khayyat ﷺ with whom he studied a part of the *Sahih* Collection of Imam al-Bukhari and the *Hikam* of Sidi Ibn 'Ata' Allah al-Iskandari ﷺ;

- Sidi Shaykh 'Abd as-Salam al-Huwari ﷺ with whom he studied *Kitab az-Zaqqaqiyya* with the commentary that the shaykh himself had written on it;

- Sidi Shaykh Khalil al-Khalidi ﷺ with whom he studied the *Alfiyya* with the commentary of al-Makuri, and *at-Tawdih* by Ibn Hisham;

- Sidi Shaykh Muhammad ibn Ja'far al-Kittani with whom he studied a section of *Jam' al-Jawami'* and part of the *Musnad* of Imam Ahmad ibn Hanbal;

- Sidi Shaykh at-Tayyib ibn Kiran ﷺ with whom he studied a section of the book, *Tawhid al-Murshid.*

- Sidi Shaykh Muhammad Kannun ﷺ with whom he studied a section of the *Mukhtasar* of al-Khalil, part of the explanation of the *Mukhtasar* of as-Sa'di and part of *Tawhid al-Murshid* with the commentary of at-Tayyib ibn Kiran;

- Sidi Shaykh Muhammad ibn 'Abd ar-Rahman al-Filali ﷺ with whom he studied [*al-Murshid*] *al-Mu'in*;

- Sidi Shaykh Hammad as-Sanhaji ﷺ with whom he studied a section of the *Mukhtasar* of Shaykh Sidi Khalil ﷺ, *ash-Shifa'* of Qadi 'Iyad ﷺ, and part of the Mayyara commentary on *Murshid al-Mu'in*;

- Sidi Shaykh Muhammad Sukayrij (Skirej) al-Ansari ﷺ, one of the scholars of the Tijaniyya *tariqa* whose love for him was so great that, when he was absent from his circle of instruction, he would cancel his lesson because our Shaykh – due to his great intelligence and strong memory – was responsible for presenting the lessons to the students after Sidi Shaykh Sukayrij had given it to them;

- Sidi Shaykh 'Abdullah ibn Idris al-Badrawi ⁂, the esteemed *faqih* and leader of the Idrisid sharifs. Our shaykh benefited from his company and studied with him the commentary of al-Qastallani on *al-Bukhari*, highlights of the *Mukhtasar* of Shaykh Khalil and *al-Isti'ara* of Shaykh at-Tayyib ibn Kiran, and highlights of the *Hamziyya* of al-Busiri with the commentary of Ibn Hajar.

When our Shaykh ⁂ finished his studies at the Qarawiyyin, he received an *ijaza* from all of his shaykhs for what he had learned from them in the areas of knowledge and fields of study that were their speciality. By that he was entitled to teach.

His teaching at the Qarawiyyin Mosque

Our Shaykh – may Allah purify his secret – volunteered to teach in the Qasba an-Nawwar mosque (in Fes) and then moved to the Qarawiyyin mosque. He had a known seat there. His lessons were divided between *fiqh* and *tafsir*. He also taught *ash-Shifa'* by Qadi 'Iyad ⁂, his preferred book for teaching the qualities of Muhammad ⁂. One thing reported about him is that he used to go to the Qarawiyyin riding on a mule reciting five *hizb*s of the Noble Qur'an on the way there. When he finished his teaching, he would ride back to his house reciting another five *hizb*s. In this way he ⁂ used to recite the entire Qur'an every six days.

In the mosque of the Qasba an-Nawwar in Fes, he used to teach *al-Murshid al-Mu'in* by Imam Sidi Ahmad ibn 'Ashir, the *Mukhtasar* of Sidi Khalil, the *Muwatta'* of Imam Malik and *Kitab al-'Aqida* of Imam as-Sanusi ⁂, in addition to his classes on *tafsir*.

Those who attended his classes at that time included the future political leaders, 'Allal al-Fasi and Sidi Muhammad al-Mukhtar as-Sanusi, the *faqih* Sidi Muhammad al-Ghazi, Qadi Sidi Muhammad ibn Qaddur, the upright *faqih* Sidi 'Abd al-Qadir as-Siqillani. Qadi Moulay Idris ibn 'Ali, Qadi Sidi as-Siddiq al-Fasi, the *faqih* Ibn 'Abdullah, director of the Makhfiya Madrasa, as well as many others also benefited from him and were trained by him. May Allah have mercy on all of them![3]

His jihad in the Cause of Allah

Morocco, like the rest of the Islamic nations, suffered from the woes of oppressive colonialism and the people of that good land could not avoid resisting it, both politically and militarily. Scholars and righteous men in Morocco rose as one to encourage the nation to fight against it, including our Shaykh ﷺ during the time he was teaching in the Qarawiyyin Mosque. He spurred on the people to fight *jihad* and called on them to resist occupation.

And he backed up his words with actions which he reinforced by joining the ranks of the *mujahidun*, despite the fact that he was not used to riding horses and had no experience of fighting. He bought a horse and weapons and hired someone to teach him how to ride, trained in ways of fighting and learned how to swim. Having done that, he bade farewell to his mother, to his teachers, to his students and all those he loved. As a *mujahid* in the Way of Allah, he joined the popular resistance forces which were led by the Darqawi zawiyas in the region of the Middle Atlas.

The shaykh was absent from his family for a long time until word spread in Fes that he had died as a martyr. His mother was deeply grieved on hearing this as he was her only child. After a time, however, he returned safe and sound after having lived through this time of jihad and proved himself in the company of *mujahidin* from every part of Morocco. When he returned, joy returned to his mother and all the people of Fes!⁴ On the battlefield he met illustrious warriors, such as the shaykh, Sidi 'Ali Muhawish (Amhaouch) ﷺ, the shaykh of the zawiya of Imhiwash, who was one of the followers of the Darqawi Tariqa, and who had great spiritual authority, extending from the tribes of the Atlas to the borders of Tafilalet.

His meeting the shaykhs of his time ﷺ

The number of scholars and gnostics whom our Shaykh, Sidi Muhammad ibn al-Habib ﷺ met is so great that the few pages of this brief biography could never list them, for all of his long life was spent in visiting and meeting the people of Allah. However, it is certainly worth mentioning some of those he met.

His meeting Sidi Ma' al-'Aynayn ﷺ

Our shaykh met the gnostic of Allah Sidi Ma' al-'Aynayn ﷺ in Fes. There was great love between the two of them. Sidi Ma' al-'Aynayn gave him an *ijaza* for all the books he had written on *hadith*, *fiqh*, *tasawwuf* and for all of his *hizb*s and *wird*s. Sidi Muhammad ibn al-Habib ﷺ said, 'I received from him (meaning Sidi Ma' al-'Aynayn) a great gift (*nafha*) and he gave me *idhn* for all the *hizb*s, Names and *wird*s with their *dhikr* and permission to give them to those who sought them.'⁵

When Sidi Ma' al-'Aynayn died and moved to the Highest Companion in 1910, our shaykh ﷺ kept close company with his *khalifa* and the inheritor of his secret, Sidi Ahmad ash-Shams, for ten years. There was a strong bond of love between them as well. Sidi Muhammad ibn al-Habib ﷺ said about him, 'I met with his *khalifa* and the inheritor of his secret, Sidi Ahmad ash-Shams, and I had a close connection of the heart with him. He used to stay with me to study different texts and I used to help him in that for close to ten years until he emigrated to Madina al-Munawwara where he died.'[6]

His meeting Sidi 'Abd ar-Rahman ibn Salih ﷺ

Our shaykh met the gnostic of Allah Almighty, Sidi 'Abd ar-Rahman ibn Salih. They discussed the true nature of servanthood (*'ubudiya*) to Allah Almighty. One thing this Shaykh ﷺ said was: 'Opening comes quickly to the true *fuqara'* when they have realised the qualities of servanthood which are: ignorance, powerlessness, weakness and poverty. If someone realises his ignorance, Allah helps him with useful knowledge. It is the same with the rest of the attributes. Realisation of your attribute results in Him supporting you with His attribute.'[7]

His meeting with Sidi Muhammad al-Ghiyathi ﷺ

From early in his life our shaykh ﷺ showed love for right-acting scholars and *awliya'* of Allah. One of those he benefited from who saw him and made supplication for him was the gnostic of Allah Almighty, Sidi Muhammad al-Ghiyathi. He said, relating about his meeting with him:

'One way that Allah has blessed me is by my meeting with many of the gnostics of Allah Almighty. Among them are those from whom I benefited by consulting them, acting on their advice and imitating their states, and those from whom I took and retained their *wird*s. One of those from whom I benefited by his seeing me and making supplication for me was the righteous shaykh, the gnostic of Allah Almighty, Sidi Muhammad al-Ghiyathi. The means of our meeting was an 'Alawi *sharif* called Moulay 'Ali who used to call the *adhan* for us at Qasba an-Nawwar (in Fes). He loved me for the sake of Allah Almighty and kept on asking me to go with him to visit him [Sidi Muhammad] which I agreed to do. When we reached the door of Sidi Muhammad al-Ghiyathi's house, he (Moulay 'Ali) knocked lightly on it and Sidi al-Ghiyathi himself came and opened it, allowing him alone to enter. Then Moulay 'Ali told him about me and that I had come to visit him out of love for Allah Almighty. He gave me permission to enter and I went in, greeted him and kissed his hand. He began to look at me and I lowered my eyes out of modesty before him and awe at his majestic presence. He asked me what I was doing and I said to him, "I have been busy with recitation of the Qur'an and now, praise be to Allah, I have memorised it and am ready to start my studies." He prayed for good for me and gave me *idhn* to recite the dhikr of *'hasbuna'llahu wa ni'm al-wakil'* a certain number of times. He was one of those who seclude themselves in their houses. He ﷺ died in the year 1318/1900.'

His meeting with Sidi 'Abdullah al-Badrawi ﷺ

The means by which our shaykh met this righteous *wali* was that Sidi 'Abdullah al-Badrawi showed great interest in him and often asked about him. He indicated to Sidi as-Siddiq ﷺ, the uncle of our Shaykh, that he was interested in him and told him that the child would have a position of great importance. Regarding his meeting with him, our Shaykh ﷺ said:

'Another of Allah's blessings to me was my meeting with the *sharif*, the *faqih* and learned scholar, the accomplished *hafiz*, the Shaykh of the Community in his time, *mawlana* 'Abdullah al-Badrawi. He was the leader of the Idrisid sharifs. The way I met him was that my uncle, Sidi as-Siddiq was one of those who used to sit with him and serve him. Sidi 'Abdullah would ask my uncle about me and say to him, "Pay attention to your nephew, Muhammad ibn al-Habib. He will be someone of immense importance."

'My uncle ordered me to visit him, and I obeyed his instruction and went to him at his house in Derb Behhaj in the Tal'a quarter of Fes. When his eyes fell on me, he began to welcome me again and again and had me sit near him. I kissed his hand and he asked me about the studies I was pursuing in the Qarawiyyin. I told him about that and he was very happy with me and made supplication for good for me. He told me to attend his morning class in which he used to teach the *Mukhtasar* of Shaykh Khalil. I did that and, by his blessing, gained a greatly increased ability to memorise. He used to read a *surah* and state what the commentators said about it, not omitting anything however rare or anomalous. He presented it with accurate memorisation, understanding and exactness. Then he continued by presenting al-Kharashi[3], following that up with the marginal commentary of as-Sa'idi[9], and the *Zawa'id* of az-Zurqani along with the margin of Banani. Then he would go into all that ar-Ruhuni[10] brought. Sometimes in addition he examined some arguments regarding it against Shaykh Banani or az-Zurqani. He supported his research with fundamental rules and texts of *fiqh* all of which attests to his vast knowledge.'[11]

His meeting with Sidi Muhammad Lahlu ﷺ

Sidi Muhammad ibn al-Habib had an intense desire to study the books of the Sufi masters such as *Ihya' 'Ulum ad-Din*, the *Hikam* of Ibn 'Ata' Allah, the *Tabaqat as-Sufiyya* of Sidi 'Abd al-Wahhab ash-Sha'rani, *al-Wasaya* of Sidi Muhyi ad-din ibn 'Arabi and other such texts. His *himma* was connected to Allah Almighty. He was constantly making supplication to Allah to connect him with someone who would help him to do that. He ﷺ said, 'I turned to the study of *'ilm* and Allah Almighty helped me with that and so in a short time I acquired a considerable quantity of such knowledge. Then in my free time I used to read books of admonition, containing reminders of death and its terrors. My heart was receptive and so fear of death was firmly fixed in my heart. I began to sleep very little at night and directed myself to prepare for death. I used to pray thirteen *rak'ats* in the night, reciting five *hizbs* with *tartil* and reflection. After that I would turn to *dhikr*, supplication and humble entreaty until the breaking of dawn. When dawn arrived, I usually went out to the mosque and prayed *Subh*, although sometimes I would pray with my family and busy myself with reciting my portion.'

This is how he spent his time ﷺ filled with *dhikr* of Allah Almighty and striving against his *nafs*, hoping that Allah would take him to someone to connect him to Him and give him direct knowledge of Him. So Allah Almighty inspired him to seek for one of the masters of hearts and gnosis of Allah in order to take his hand, his heart being ready for the station of *ihsan* which includes watchfulness (*muraqaba*) of Allah and witnessing of Him (*mushahada*) as is found in the text in the hadith of Jibril ﷺ related by al-Bukhari and Muslim. When Jibril ﷺ asked the Prophet ﷺ

about *ihsan* he replied, '*Ihsan* is that you worship Allah as if you were seeing Him. Even if you do not see Him, He sees you.' There is no doubt that someone who yearns to taste this station only reaches it by means of a guide who is a gnostic of Allah and the first such man our Shaykh benefited from at the beginning of his path was the shaykh and gnostic of Allah, the one annihilated in the love of the *awliya'* of Allah, Sidi Muhammad Lahlu ﷺ. This gnostic of Allah was head of the tanning guild of Fes.[12]

Our Shaykh ﷺ spoke about his meeting with him:

'Pursuit of knowledge became a burden for me and worship and devotion to Allah Almighty became easy for me. I said to myself, "The goal of knowledge is action. I have obtained the amount of knowledge necessary for me, so why should I concern myself with anything in excess of that? I am not a *mufti* or a *qadi*." I felt great bewilderment and was in need of Allah Almighty to give me someone to take my hand and guide me to the path of good. While I was in this state of bewilderment, I passed through Zuqaq al-Hajar and my eye fell upon this sayyid (Sidi Muhammad Lahlu). There was a light coming from him that stretched upwards from his head, rising towards heaven, which I thought that must be visible to everyone. I followed him and found that that light was not being seen by anyone else. So I knew that Allah Almighty had let me see something of his elite status (*khususiyya*) while veiling it from other people. My heart was set on joining him.

'My uncle, Sidi as-Siddiq, was his brother in Allah Almighty. So I went to him and told him what had happened to me and what Allah Almighty had shown me about his elite status. He said to me, "That is a man who has received opening. He meets together with men of the elite and has served them with diligence, truthfulness, intention and love. That is why he has acquired immense light and great good." So I asked him to take me to him so that I could inform him of my state of bewilderment. He helped me and arranged a meeting for me at midday of the following day in my uncle's house in the quarter of Sidi 'Abd al-Qadir al-Fasi. When the appointed time came, I went but did not find him. I said to my uncle, "Where is this sayyid?" He told me, "He will certainly come."

'My uncle went out to meet him and found him at the door. When he entered, he said to my uncle, "Sidi as-Siddiq, shall we sit in downstairs or upstairs?" He answered, "We have prepared upstairs for the meeting." He said to him, "You can only ascend to what is higher by climbing up the rungs of the ladder. Anyone who wants to ascend without a ladder will not achieve his goal." This was the first *ishara* (spiritual allusion) I heard from him and I knew that what I had to do was ascend step by step and travel at the hand of the people of opening and light. When he came up and reached the room where I was waiting for him, I stood up showing great *adab* and greeted him and he sat close to me and turned to me with full attention and great aspiration (*himma*).'

Our Shaykh ﷺ remained in the company of Sidi Muhammad Lahlu ﷺ for five years. He used to meet with him together with five[i] of the brothers for *dhikr* and discussion (*mudhākara*) for the sake of Allah Almighty. He used to tell them to reflect on the *ayah*: '*The Day when neither wealth nor sons will be of any use – except to those who come to Allah with sound and flawless hearts.*'

---

i These five who used to meet included Sidi Sa'id al-Belghithi as will be mentioned. He taught them the *wird* of Sidi al-'Arabi ibn 'Abdullah al-Huwari.

(26:87-88) Among other things that Sidi Muhammad Lahlu advocated was to have high esteem for the *awliya'* of Allah, to seek excuses for the slaves of Allah, to honour scholars and students and all of those whom Allah has put in charge of the affairs of the Muslims and to pray for good for them. Our Shaykh learned these precepts from him and adopted them, called people to them and taught them to his *murid*s.

His taking the tariqa of Sidi al-'Arabi ibn 'Abdullah Baba al-Huwari ﷺ

When Shaykh Sidi Muhammad al-'Arabi al-Madighri ﷺ died,[i] a

---

i   Sidi Muhammad ibn al-'Arabi al-Madighri, born in 1216/1801, was a descendant of a noble family. He studied at the Qarawiyyin Mosque in Fes. After a lengthy period of seeking knowledge, he returned to the land of M'dghara on the left bank of the Middle Ziz. He was burning with yearning to spread what was feasible for him of knowledge and gnosis among his family, especially the Darqawi Sufi teaching he had experienced in Fes. Close to his birthplace he founded the Darqawi zawiya known as Rahmatullah and then he founded a second zawiya in Tafilalt, south of Safalat: the zawiya of Gawz, near the historical Kasr Tinghras. His reputation spread and students and murids came to him from all parts of southeastern Morocco and the southwest of Algeria. His fame reached the lands of Egypt and Mesopotamia. People from Baghdad visited him in the Rahmatullah zawiya, to learn from him and drink from his fount of knowledge. He was unique in his region for his followers and fame and his students were numbered in the thousands. His zawiya was prominent in the popular resistance against the French occupation in southeastern Morocco. Indeed, it was a stronghold for the Algerian mujahidin. Among them we mention the mujahid, Shaykh Buamama who met with Shaykh Sidi Muhammad ibn al-'Arabi on an annual basis. He died – may Allah purify his secret – in 1309/1892 in his zawiya in the village of Gawz in the province of Errachidia. His tomb is well known there. He, may Allah be number of his murids whom he left as shaykhs went out to teach. Praise be to Allah. They included his daughter's husband, Shaykh Moulay al-Hasan, Shaykh Sidi as-Siddiq al-Qaddari in Tafilalet, Shaykh Sidi al-'Arabi ibn 'Abdullah Baba al-Huwari,[i] Shaykh Sidi 'Abd al-Malik, Shaykh Sidi Moulay Ahmad as-Sab'i, Shaykh Sidi Muhammad ibn Ahmad in Sefrou (in the district of Fez), Shaykh Sidi Brik ibn Qasba an-Nuwwar, Shaykh Sidi Muhammad al-Hajj in the region of Zemmour, Shaykh Sidi at-Tayyib ibn 'Abd al-Malik, Shaykh Sidi 'Ali ibn al-Makki of Muhawshi, and Shaykh Sidi Muhammad ibn 'Ali in Marrakesh.

Sidi Moulay as-Sa'id al-Belghithi ﷺ agreed with one of the *sharifs* to go on hajj, turning his back on the disagreement which

---

pleased with him, left more than forty-three zawiyas spread through Dadis, Todgha, Ferkla, M'dghara, ar-Reteb, Boudnib, and most of the Filali qsars (around the jihad abodes of the Darqawi tariqa and Sufi scholars in Tafilalt). See Muhammad Bukabut, *Muqāwama al-hawāmish as-sahrawīya lil-isti'mār (1880-1938): unknown pages from the masters of the tribes of the eastern borders of Tafilalt to Wadi Nul*, Dar Abi Raqraq publishing, Rabat, 2005.

i   Sidi al-'Arabi ibn 'Abdullah Baba al-Huwari. He was the spiritual Qutb, the shaykh of the Tariqa and the noble knight of the *haqiqa*. He took from Shaykh Sidi Muhammad al-'Arabi al-Madighri who was the muqaddam of Shaykh Sidi Ahmad al-Badawi Zwitan, may Allah be pleased with all of them. He founded his zawiya beside the zawiya of his father, Sidi 'Abdullah Baba al-Huwari in Ferkla in 1273/1857 while his father was still alive. At that time he was the *muqaddam* of Sidi Ahmad al-Badawi Zwitan. He became a shaykh after the death of his shaykh, Sidi Muhammad al-'Arabi al-Madighri in 1892. He had many miracles (*karamāt*), including the earth being rolled up to shorten the distance. He was a contemporary of Sultan Moulay 'Abd al-'Aziz and Sultan Moulay al-Hasan I ibn Muhammad, may Allah have mercy on all of them. They used to esteem him and honour him. He died in Ferkla in the Moroccan desert in 1321/1902 and his grave is known in his zawiya there.

had occurred between the people of the region of Waqqa, some of whom did not believe in the shaykhhood of Sidi al-ʿArabi ibn ʿAbdullah al-Huwari. They went to Shaykh Sidi Muhammad ibn Ahmad (who was one of the shaykhs who was left to them by Sidi Muhammad al-ʿArabi al-Madighri in the region of Sefrou in the district of Fes). The two of them wanted him to intercede for them with the wazir, Ubba Ahmad, so that he would give them a boat ticket to enable them to travel to the Holy lands to perform the obligation of hajj. When they reached him, he met them and welcomed them. They told him that they wanted to perform hajj and he ﷺ answered them (in colloquial Moroccan): 'I don't think you're going on hajj, but if you have the money, give it to me so that I can spend it on the *fuqara'* (the *murids*).'

That night Moulay as-Saʿid al-Belghithi had a dream in which it seemed that a breast emerged from Shaykh Sidi Muhammad ibn Ahmad from which he drank sweet milk. When he woke up, he recounted this dream to his friend, the *sharif*. They agreed that they would renew the *bayʿa* with Shaykh Sidi Muhammad ibn Ahmad, believing that he was the shaykh with *idhn*. After the *Fajr* prayer, they bent to kiss him and asked him to take their hands for Allah. He said to them, 'Glory be to Allah! You, people of Waqqa (the name of their town), what has happened to you is the same as what happened to the man who was with a water-carrier (a man who carries a skin of water on his shoulder from which people can drink and rings a bell to let them know he is there). He left him and went to someone who had neither waterskin nor bell and said to him, "Give me water!" It is Shaykh Sidi al-ʿArabi ibn ʿAbdullah Baba al-Huwari ﷺ who has the waterskin, saying, "Water for the road! Water for the road!" ... Go to him and give *baʿya* to him.'

In the evening he said to the two of them, 'Sidi al-Hashimi, the brother of Shaykh Sidi al-'Arabi ibn 'Abdullah al-Huwari, is with us in Sefrou and he is intending to travel to the desert.' So Sidi Moulay as-Sa'id al-Belghithi took the opportunity and wrote a letter to Sidi al-'Arabi ibn 'Abdullah al-Huwari, saying in it that he wanted to renew the *ba'ya* at his hand. He gave the letter to Sidi al-Hashimi, the brother of Sidi al-'Arabi ibn 'Abdullah, along with a gift of money to accompany it. A week later, Sidi al-Hashimi returned to Sefrou with a letter from Shaykh Sidi al-'Arabi ibn 'Abdullah al-Huwari 🌿 in which he said, after the *basmala* and praise of Allah: 'Your letter, visit, and request for *idhn* reached us. You are worthy of it. We have given you *idhn* to recite it (meaning the *wird*) as we recited it with Shaykh Sidi Muhammad al-'Arabi al-Madighri 🌿 and we have also given you *idhn* to teach the *wird* to anyone who asks for it from you; but only give it to those who seek it and persist in seeking it. It is more precious to us than the blackness of our eyes.'

So Sidi as-Sa'id al-Belghithi renewed the pledge with Sidi al-'Arabi ibn 'Abdullah al-Huwari and had *idhn* from him to receive the *ba'ya* from those who asked for it when they met its preconditions. When it came time for the hajj, the wazir Ubba Ahmad had died and it was not possible for Sidi as-Sa'id al-Belghithi and his companion to perform hajj just as Shaykh Sidi Muhammad ibn Ahmad had foretold for them, so Moulay Sa'id went to Fes and his *sharif* companion returned to the desert. One day Moulay as-Sa'id al-Belghithi entered the Qarawiyyin mosque and found Sidi Muhammad Lahlu 🌿 with a group of *fuqara'* doing *dhikr* of Allah. They included Sidi Muhammad ibn al-Habib 🌿. He was the youngest of them. Moulay as-Sa'id sat with them and they asked him about the life and spiritual states of Shaykh Sidi Muhammad al-'Arabi al-Madighri. He answered them because he had been one of his scribes and had kept his company for a long time. They spoke at length about his excellent blessing and yearned to take *ba'ya* with him.

Before he met Sidi as-Sa'id, whenever Sidi Muhammad Lahlu wanted to take *ba'ya* with someone, one of his shaykhs would come to him in a dream and stop him. When he met Sidi Moulay as-Sa'id and listened to his words, his state was moved and his yearning strengthened. Moulay as-Sa'id related the story of him receiving the *ba'ya* of Muhammad Lahlu: 'One day I was sitting after the *'Asr* prayer on the roof of the zawiya in Fes and heard the sound of someone coming. It was Sidi Muhammad Lahlu. He greeted me and said to me, "I want the *wird*." I answered him, "There are many shaykhs. Go to them and take it from one of them. Go to Shaykh Muhammad ibn Ahmad in Sefrou and take it from him. There is also Sidi Brik in Qasba an-Nuwwar. There is also Sidi Muhammad al-Hajj in Zemmour." When he heard my words, he left.'

After the *Maghrib* prayer, [Sidi Moulay as-Sa'id said,] 'I informed the *fuqara'* about what had happened between me and Sidi Muhammad Lahlu and they said, "By Allah, Sidi, only *adab* on his part kept him from taking it from you." I said to them, "Shaykh Sidi al-'Arabi ibn 'Abdullah Baba al-Huwari ﷺ told me to only give the *wird* to those who persisted in asking for it. If Sidi Muhammad Lahlu is truthful in his quest, he will return and insist on asking for it. The following day at the same time and at the same place, Sidi Muhammad Lahlu came quickly and said to me, "My resolve is strong." I answered him the same way I had done the day before and he repeated, "My resolve is strong. Who will guarantee for me that death will not delay me if I leave with you telling me, 'Go to Sefrou. Go to Zemmour.'" When I heard these words from him, I knew that he was truthful and I recited the beginning of the *wird* to him and gave him *idhn* for it.

'After that he invited me for an evening meal. When I entered his house, he told his companions were sitting there (which included Sidi Muhammad ibn al-Habib), "I inform you that I have taken the *wird* of Sidi Shaykh al-'Arabi ibn 'Abdullah al-Huwari. That is so that you do not say that I have betrayed you." They all answered him, "Sayyiduna, we yearn for that and nothing kept us from giving the pledge to Sidi Moulay as-Sa'id other than showing proper *adab* with you." Then they all took the *wird* from me in the house of Sidi Muhammad. In the morning Sidi Muhammad came to me and described Sidi al-'Arabi al-Huwari to me. It was as if he were looking at him. I said to him, "What did you see? What did he say to you?" He answered, "I dreamt that it was as if I had a daughter whom I gave to him and I asked him, 'How was she with you, Sidi?' He answered, 'We found her to be polished and well-mannered. When she was haughty, we said to her, "Allah is greater! How small you are!"'"

'When I heard this true dream from him, I said to him, "Sidi Muhammad. That is your *nafs* which you have given to Shaykh Sidi al-'Arabi al-Huwari. Praise be to Allah that he found is it polished and well-mannered!"[i]

---

i   The story in full was told to me by Sidi Muhammad ibn Sidi Muhammad Belqurshi, the muqaddam of the zawiya of Touroug (in the south of Morocco)

Renewal of the pledge to Sidi Muhammad ibn 'Ali 🕮

So our Shaykh 🕮 remained earnestly striving in the Darqawi Tariqa until the gnostic of Allah, Sidi Muhammad ibn 'Ali 🕮[i] appeared in Marrakesh and he took *ba'ya* with him and followed his blessed Tariqa. He 🕮 mentioned the story of the renewal of his *ba'ya* with him, saying: 'When he, i.e. Sidi Muhammad ibn 'Ali, took charge, I wrote a letter to him to renew the *ba'ya* with him after I had taken the Tariqa with the gnostic Shaykh, Sidi al-'Arabi ibn al-Huwari. He 🕮 wrote and told me to come to his presence. I obeyed his command and went to Marrakesh. When I visited him 🕮, he was filled with limitless joy and happiness. He said to me. "All of the Order came when you came to me."[13] Then he gave him the good news of what his business would lead to and said to him, 'You are with us in our Order as Ibn 'Ata' Allah is in the Shadhili *tariqa*. As Allah revived the Shadhiliya *tariqa* through Ibn 'Ata' Allah, so Allah will revive this blessed *tariqa* through you, Allah willing.'[14]

---

from his father Sidi Muhammad Belqurshi who heard it from his shaykh, Moulay as-Sa'id al-Belghithi, may Allah be pleased with all of them and give us the benefit of their knowledge and secrets!

i He is Abu 'Abdullah Sidi Muhammad (Fatha) ibn 'Ali ad-Dar'i al-Firkli. He was a clear full moon at whose hands miracles (*karamat*) appeared. One of them was related by Sidi Belqurshi. He looked for a water-carrier and one did not come to him, so he took a stone and threw it into a well in his house whose water was salty and it immediately became sweet. At the beginning of his journey on the Path he put on the *muraqqa'a* (patched garment) and tied the middle of it with a strap and at the end of his life rode on fine horses and wore the finest garments. He had a zawiya which was built while he was alive and he had followers. He died on the morning of Tuesday, 12 Rabi' al-Awwal 1326/1908 and is buried in the middle of his zawiya.

Our master, Shaykh Sidi Muhammad ibn al-Habib 🕮 remained in the zawiya of Sidi Muhammad ibn 'Ali 🕮 for four years. When he first arrived in the zawiya of Sidi Muhammad ibn 'Ali, whenever food was brought to the murids, he divided his portion of meat between those of the *murids* who ate with him. Sidi Muhammad ibn 'Ali observed him doing this although our master, the Shaykh, was not aware of that. On the fourth day he called to him and asked him, 'Why do you give away your portion of meat, Sidi Muhammad, and not eat it?' Sayyiduna Shaykh answered. 'Sidi, I used to want to eat and my self told me that I should take the largest portion of meat so I wanted to oppose its desire by depriving it of eating meat totally.' Sidi Muhammad ibn 'Ali was delighted by this answer and said, 'You have taken everything, my son. You have taken everything.'[15]

His appearance as a shaykh and calling to the path of the People of Allah

When Shaykh Sidi Muhammad ibn 'Ali had observed in our Shaykh 🕮 the signs of knowledge and righteousness he began to order him to engage in discussion (*mudhakara*) with the fuqara' on necessary knowledge in the *deen*. He used to present the *Murshid al-Mu'in* and then followed it by presenting the *Kitab al-Munajat al-Kubra* by Sidi Ahmad al-Badawi 🕮.[i] Our Shaykh

---

i   Sidi Ahmad al-Badawi ibn Ahmad al-Fasi Zwitan who was born in the city of Fes in the eighteenth century and died in 1275/1858. He studied knowledge with the shaykhs of Fes in his time. They included at-Tayyib ibn Kiran, Hamdun ibn al-Hajj and 'Abd as-Salam al-Azmi. After he had obtained a portion of outward knowledge, he directed himself to Sufism and joined his shaykh, Moulay al-'Arabi ad-Darqawi, the Shaykh of the Darqawiyya tariqa

said about it: 'This book contains everything that is needed by the one who seeks the station of *Ihsan*. Among the things its author ﷺ said is: "Every one of the *awliya'* of Allah Almighty enters by the door which Allah Almighty has opened for him. I entered by the door of esteem for the creatures of Allah Almighty and my guide in this is the words of Allah: *'That is it. So for those who honour Allah's sacred rites, that comes from the taqwa in their hearts.'* (22:22) So esteem for the People of the House settled in my heart and I did not see a *sharif* without esteem for him settling in my heart so that it was as if I was seeing the Prophet ﷺ. When I saw a scholar, esteem for him settled in my heart and the light which he had taken from the Prophet ﷺ flooded over me. I had esteem for all the Muslims since they are slaves of Allah Almighty and I saw myself as the least of all of them until I began to esteem the entire universe since it is known by Divine Knowledge and is the effect of His specific will, the projection of His power and the perfection of His wisdom. Glory be to Him and exalted is He!"'[16]

Our Shaykh ﷺ travelled with his teacher, Sidi Muhammad ibn 'Ali ﷺ on a number of his journeys. Regarding the last of them he said about himself: 'Then I remained on this journey for close to two months. When we reached the Saraghina tribe and they were happy with the Shaykh and all the brothers, he ordered me to return to Fes to represent him in guiding to Allah. He

---

before 1810. He took the tariqa from him. He worked as a merchant and he had a shop in the market of perfumers in Fes in addition to acting as imam in the Sharabiliyyin Mosque. He became a Sufi Shaykh and instructed *murids* in the Darqawi tariqa in his zawiya in Fes. See his biography in the book of Shaykh 'Abdullah ibn 'Abd al-Qadir at-Talidi, *al-Mu'rib fi mashahir awliya' al-Maghrib*, Dar al-Aman, Ribat, fourth edition 2003, p. 233.

taught me the Unique Name (*al-Ism al-Mufrad*) and commanded me to do *dhikr* with it often in a specific manner which he had learned from his shaykh, Sidi Ahmad al-Badawi. It is reflected in the words of Ibn 'Ata' Allah in his *Hikam*: "If it were not for His manifestation in beings, no eye could see them." There is no doubt that He is manifest in beings by what this Name contains of knowledge of the Essence of Allah, His Attributes and Names, and His Actions by which the effects of His Names and Attributes are made manifest. They are called 'beings'.

'Shaykh 'Abd al-Wahhab ash-Shadhili ﷺ said, "There is nothing in existence except what He already knows, and has been singled out by Will, put in place by Power and arranged by Wisdom." Sidi Ibn 'Ata' Allah ﷺ said in another wisdom of the *Hikam*: "Phenomenal being is utter and total darkness. It is only the manifestation of the Real in it that gives it light. When you see phenomenal being and do not see Him (Allah) in it, with it, before it or after it, then you are truly in need of light. You are veiled from the suns of gnoses by the clouds of secondary traces." I used to do a lot of *dhikr* of this Name while recalling this, and by the blessing of this Name my heart was illuminated and I arrived at that watchfulness (*muraqaba*) of Allah and witnessing (*mushahada*) of Him which characterises the station of *ihsan*, and is expressed in the words of the hadith: "that you worship Allah as if you could see Him. Even if you do not see Him, He sees you.'" He ﷺ said, 'It is in the hadith of Jibril. When he ﷺ was asked about the one who asked, he said, "That was Jibril who came to teach you your *deen*." So the Prophet ﷺ called Islam, *iman* and *ihsan* the *deen*. In short, the Sufi path is based on obtaining knowledge of the station of *ihsan* and this knowledge requires a guide (*murshid*) as every knowledge has a guide who explains its rules and technical terms. This is what moved me to seek a guide.'[17]

His role ⌘ as a teaching Shaykh began in 1908, which was when his shaykh Sidi Muhammad ibn 'Ali ⌘ died. He was 37 years old at that time. He continued to hesitate to declare himself for some time, preferring to remain hidden and obscure, until one day he dreamt of his beloved ancestor the Chosen One ⌘ who gave him a command which left him no choice but to make himself known and openly guide people to Allah. That is why we prefer to give the starting date of his shaykhdom in a clear form as 1911 when he had reached the age of forty, as is stated by some of those who relate his biography. He himself ⌘ spoke about that, saying: 'When Shaykh Sidi Muhammad ibn 'Ali ⌘ died (i.e. in 1908) and *idhn* was confirmed for me, I thought little of myself and that I was not worthy of that station. Then the four shaykhs came to me. They were: Sidi Muhammad ibn 'Ali ⌘, Sidi al-'Arabi ibn al-Huwari ⌘, Sidi Muhammad al-'Arabi (al-Madighri) ⌘ and Sidi Ahmad al-Badawi (Zwitan) ⌘. They commanded me to go forth to people and guide them to Allah and said, "The water which you drank from us is the coolest and sweetest water. Stretch out your hand to the east and west and do not fear anyone."

'Then after that *idhn* came to me from the Chosen One ⌘ and there was a threat telling me I had to go forth. So I went forth to people by Allah and for Allah.'[18] Good tidings from the presence of the Prophet continued to come to him ⌘. An example of that is what he said about the sweet waters which he drank when speaking about the blessings of Allah Almighty to him. He said, 'He (the Prophet) ⌘ gave me good tidings by saying to me: "My son, know that Allah honours you by giving you sweet and pleasant waters to drink." I said, "Messenger of Allah, are these waters the waters of Islam, *Iman* and *Ihsan*?" "They are," he ﷺ answered me. I asked, "Messenger of Allah, will I drink these waters alone or are they for me and all those who follow me?" He replied, "You will drink them as well as all of my community who follow you." Allah realised for us what the Prophet ﷺ promised us. By Allah, we drank from these waters and all who accompany us with truthfulness will drink them in the shortest space of time. So praise Allah, my masters, and thank Him for how He has honoured your master in your time.'[19] He also said, 'The shaykh of our Shaykh, Sidi Muhammad al-'Arabi (al-Madighri) ﷺ, said, "Allah only brings me someone who is accepted." I say, speaking by the blessings of Allah, "Allah will only bring me someone who is beloved."'[20]

That is how it is with the state of the truthful shaykhs. They only appear to people by Allah and for Allah after clear explicit *idhn* from the greatest intermediary, the presence of the Beloved Chosen One, our master Muhammad ﷺ. That is so that their guidance of people is a Divine Muhammadan guidance, safe from any incentive of fame or personal fortune and protected from the evils of rivalry for worldly desires, supported and protected by the eye of divine concern. There was indescribable love and acceptance for him in every region he traversed with his noble feet. He was like the abundant rain. It benefits wherever it falls. He spoke about *baraka* and the secret of *idhn*, saying, 'By Allah, and again by Allah, we did not pass through any city, village or desert without its people witnessing the arrival of succour to them and the increase of life flowing in their hearts. That is the secret of *idhn*. Praise be to Allah, no *faqir* has sat with us without gaining a knowledge he did not have before, and through it obtaining humility and contrition. No murid of the *tariqa* sat with us without his inward being strengthened and his *himma* elevated to seeking gnosis of Allah, and no shaykh of the time did not have tasting added to his own tasting and benefit by gaining something from us which he did not have before. All of that is part of the secret and *baraka* of *idhn*.'[21]

The opening of his zawiya in Meknes

After he ﷺ returned from the hajj, he saw that his zawiya in Fes was not large enough for the murids and thought about establishing a new zawiya. He asked the *faqih*, Sidi az-Zarhuni ﷺ to look for a large house for him in Meknes which he could use as a zawiya. That *faqih* found a large house that was under the control of the Makhzan. It had been the dwelling of one of the Pashas. He spoke to those with authority over it and they agreed to sell it to him. So in 1936 our master the Shaykh bought it for the sum of 13,000 rials. He obtained this amount by selling some of the land he had inherited from his father and from his own savings.

An extraordinary event took place before *Sayyidina* Shaykh moved to Meknes. It was that he ﷺ visited Meknes with one of his murids and went to the tomb of the righteous *wali*, Sidi Sa'id ibn 'Uthman ﷺ with the intention of meeting there one of the *awliya'* of Allah called Sidi Mansur ﷺ. He brought him a gift of an article of clothing, intending to ask this *wali* to give him a spiritual drink. When he went in to the place where Sidi Mansur was, before he could say anything this righteous *wali* pre-empted him, saying, "Put the gift there." He took a glass of tea and offered it to *Sayyidina* Shaykh and said to him, "This is the drink you came for." When *Sayyidina* Shaykh drank the glass of tea, his state changed and he left him, calling out the Name of Majesty very loudly until he reached the square of al-Heddim (in the middle of Meknes). Sidi Qasim al-Hilali, who had been his friend before in the company of Sidi Muhammad Lahlu, saw him and took him by the hand and brought him to his house.

After our Shaykh's state had calmed a little, Sidi Qasim al-Hilali asked him to spend the night with him and called Sidi ar-Zarhuni, one of the *fuqaha'*, to acquaint him with what had happened. After they had together gone over some matters of *fiqh* and Sufism, this *faqih* was amazed at our shaykh and asked him to take his hand. But our shaykh refused because this *faqih* was affiliated with another *tariqa* and was a *muqaddam* in it. But Sidi az-Zarhuni persisted in asking for it and he informed *Sayyidina* Shaykh that his affiliation to that *tariqa* was just one of seeking *baraka* since he was not being taught at the hand of a living shaykh. When this was made clear, *Sayyidina* Shaykh welcomed him and accepted his *ba'ya* and appointed him as the first *muqaddam* of the *Habibiyya Tariqa* in Meknes. Sidi az-Zarhuni undertook his duties in the best fashion. He founded the first gathering of *fuqara'* in Meknes. At first they used to meet in the mosque located in Derb al-Fityan. *Sayyidina* Shaykh used to visit them there often and then he instructed the *muqaddam* Sidi az-Zarhuni to look for a place for a *zawiya* for him.

As we mentioned previously, this *faqih* actually found the appropriate place and from then on the Habibiyya zawiya in Meknes was established, *Sayyidina* Shaykh having remained in his *zawiya* in Fes for twenty-six years. This new *zawiya*, like the previous one, became a shelter for seekers of knowledge and a centre for the purification of souls. Its fame became widespread and people travelled to it from far and wide. Through it Allah brought many dead selves and moribund hearts to life. People came to it one after another from Morocco and elsewhere and at his hands about sixty foreigners, mostly from England, became Muslim.

His bringing about a rebirth in knowledge in Meknes

Our Shaykh found that the city of Meknes was in pressing need of a rebirth of knowledge, so he resolved to ask his Majesty, King Muhammad V to start an institute of higher education there. He consulted some of the great men of Meknes and they indicated to him that he should not rush into this matter. So he did an *istikhara* prayer to Allah to ask for guidance in what he had resolved to do and then went to his majesty the King. He said to him, 'You have established a religious and scholarly institute in Marrakesh yet Meknes is the capital of your ancestor so you should give it precedence.' The King answered him by saying that Fes and Meknes, being so close together were virtually one place.' Sayyiduna ash-Shaykh replied that even though that was the case, students who qualified in Fes and returned to Meknes often had to busy themselves with earning a living in other occupations so that the learning they had acquired went to waste and the people of Meknes who desired knowledge had no one to teach them.' This argument was accepted by his Majesty the King and our shaykh created a systematic plan represented by the following:[22]

- Establishing teaching places in the Zitouna Mosque in Meknes;

- Arranging that teaching according to the different scholarly levels;
- Beginning teaching by rotation inside these levels.

So our Shaykh 🙶 participated in reviving the teaching of Islamic knowledge in Meknes and he himself began to teach in the Zitouna Mosque in Meknes. Recounting the blessings of Allah he had received, he 🙶 spoke about this matter, saying, 'Then I began to teach in the Zitouna Mosque,[i] and we began by studying *tafsir*, attended by a large number of seekers of knowledge and others, and then followed that with the *Risala* of [Ibn] Abi Zayd 🙶 in the same gathering. The people of Meknes benefited from that. Praise be to Allah! For the common people of Meknes I added something from the *Murshid al-Mu'in*. And for the people of *tariqa* in Meknes I would go over the *Hikam* of Ibn 'Ata' Allah.'[23]

His connection with Sidi Ahmad ibn 'Aliwa (al-'Alawi) 🙶

Between Shaykh Sidi Muhammad ibn al-Habib and the gnostic of Allah, Sidi Ahmad ibn 'Aliwa al-Mustaghanimi[ii] there was a strong tie and pure love which was evident in the frequent visits and many letters between the two of them. One of the manifestations of the scholarly connection between the two shaykhs was that Sidi Muhammad ibn al-Habib asked Sidi Ibn 'Aliwa 🙶 to write a commentary on the prayer called the *Treasury of Truths* which he had received directly from the presence of the Prophet 🙵. Shaykh

---

i   This mosque is located close to his zawiya in Meknes.

ii   He is the Shaykh of the Shadili Darqawi 'Alawi tariqa in Algeria, 1869-1934.

al-Alawi responded to his request and devoted an entire book to it entailed *Dawhat al-Asrar fi ma'na as-Salat 'ala al-Mukhtar* 🌼.

He 🌼 said in its foreword: 'I begin by addressing the one who was the reason for me writing this book. He is the true truthful one, our brother in Allah, Sidi Muhammad ibn al-Habib ibn Mawlana as-Siddiq. May Allah make us and you among those who are true to the contract they made with Allah.

'Sidi, after seeking blessing in your qualities and asking about the totality of your states and peace which encompasses you as merit, I was greatly honoured by the receipt of your letter. It is as if it was a whole book from someone who is wise and learned. So I let my eyes peruse it and I thought deeply about it and found it to be a fertile meadow and a thing of comprehensive beauty. It is proof enough of the quality of its writer, especially given the account of the Prophetic dream to its author which it contains, may the best prayer and purest greeting be upon him. It is a great boon which we are obliged to be thankful for. Praise be to Allah for the continued existence of those like you. As for what you requested us to do with regard to clarifying the contents of the prayer which Allah made flow on your tongue, Allah knows best, but we cannot do more than you yourself have done. However I will speak in order to obey your command, serve you and benefit by the blessing of the prayer on the Prophet 🌼, acknowledging my total incapacity in all ways.'[24] Then he continued with the commentary.

Shaykh Sidi Muhammad ibn al-Habib 🌼 had drunk deeply and extensively from the source of Divine knowledge and had multiple openings to all manner of spiritual experience and he desired to teach others of the openings and gifts which Allah generously bestows on His *awliya'*. Evidence of that is contained in a letter he sent to his brother in Allah Shaykh Sidi Ahmad ibn ʿAliwa ﷺ. In it he acquainted Shaykh al-ʿAlawi with the circumstances of his becoming a shaykh and asked him to write him a letter outlining the knowledge Allah had given him connected to the practice of *khalwa,* specifying his methodology of doing *dhikr* of the Greatest Name (*al-Ismuʾl-ʿAdhm*) and asked him for an *ijaza* for it. He also indicated to Shaykh al-ʿAlawi the specific form of *dhikr* which he had received from his shaykh, Sidi Muhammad ibn ʿAli ﷺ. This was out of a desire to learn the different modes and methods of *dhikr* and *suluk* that gnostics utilise. He ended the letter by inviting Shaykh al-Alawi to visit him in Fes. And, indeed, Shaykh al-Alawi did visit Fes twice, once in 1924 and then again in 1928.

It is also important to note that our Shaykh visited Shaykh Sidi Ibn ʿAliwa in 1934 in Mostaghanem right at the end of his life when he was ill. He gave him permission to visit him while he was in a comatose state and no one else was allowed to visit him. When he came into the place where he was, Shaykh al-Alawi, who had been unconscious for some time, revived. They remained alone for a period of time and no one knew what passed between them. What some elite murids of Sidi Muhammad ibn al-Habib related is that during this encounter Shaykh Sidi Ibn ʿAliwa said to our Shaykh that he had two matters he wanted to talk to him about. The first was that he had spent a long time in refuting deniers which had diverted him from *dhikrullah* and he feared to meet Allah with that heedlessness in his record. So our Shaykh answered that what he had said and written when doing this was not heedlessness at all but was rather jihad in the Cause of Allah and defending the people of Allah and supporting them, and that far from being in any way blameworthy would, for that reason, be a cause of reward for him.

Sidi Ibn 'Aliwa 🌼 was delighted to hear that and said to him, 'Sidi, you have given me good news and brought joy to my heart. I give you the good news of a long life.' Then he advised him to spend most of his time travelling and meeting the *fuqara* wherever they were and to spend only a little time in his *zawiya*. Then he gave him a spiritual indication, saying: 'Keep the rynd[i] of the millstone after me.' The good news he gave of a long life for Sidi Muhammad ibn al-Habib 🌼 was certainly fully realised since he was over a hundred years old when he died. And throughout all of that long life he acted in accordance with the counsel he had received from Sidi Ibn 'Aliwa 🌼, travelling ceaselessly to visit his zawiyas in every region of Morocco and Algeria to teach and guide his murids and those he loved, never spending more than a few weeks at a time in his zawiya in Meknes. This continued right up to the end of his life, in spite of his great age and at times frail health, to the point that he was in Algeria on his way to hajj when the time of his death finally arrived.[ii]

His pedagogical method

At the beginning of his mission to call to the path of the people of Allah from his zawiya in Qasba al-Nuwwar in Fes – which was a centre to which the hearts of those thirsty for knowledge and yearning for instruction and wayfaring (*suluk*) were drawn – our Shaykh 🌼 himself was in charge of the teaching of the sciences

---

i The iron rod supporting the millstone.

ii I heard this account in the Habibiyya zawiya in Laghouat directly from the mouth of Sidi al-Hajj al-Miloud Chantuf 🌼, one of the elite students of Shaykh Sidi Muhammad ibn al-Habib 🌼.

of the *deen* and Arabic in addition to the teaching of the murids who desired the station of *ihsan*. He also gave general lessons in *fiqh* and *tafsir* in the Qarawiyyin Mosque.

He 🌸 said, describing his method of teaching and spreading knowledge: 'Then when this Shaykh who had acquainted me with the station of *ihsan*, namely Sidi Muhammad ibn 'Ali 🌸, died, people came to me and I began to remind them, guide them and advise them according to their capacity and predisposition without desire or innovation. We met with the brothers in *dhikr* and discussion about the Book of Allah Almighty. I would order a student with a good voice to recite a portion of the Noble Qur'an for us and he would recite *ayah*s which encourage the remembrance of Allah and reflection on the wonders of Allah's creation such as: *"...those who remember Allah, standing, sitting and lying on their sides, and reflect on the creation of the heavens and the earth: 'Our Lord, You have not created this for nothing. Glory to You! So safeguard us from he punishment of the Fire'"* (3:191) and His words: *"You who believe! remember Allah much, and glorify Him in the morning and the evening."* (33:41-42) Then there would be discussion according to those present so that each person could take his share of the meaning of the *ayah*.'[25]

He 🌸 was responsible for providing the murids, students and *fuqara* with all that they needed. He did not oblige any of those who sought knowledge with him to join his *tariqa*, as he was eager for the pure *shari'a*. His pious student, Sidi Muhammad 'Ayyat 🌸, the *muqaddam* of the *tariqa* in the city of Oran in Algeria, related that they once did a *hadra* late into the night in the Meknes zawiya and then overslept, delaying their performance of the *Subh* prayer. *Sayyidina* Shaykh looked through a window from his quarters in the upper story of the *zawiya* and himself gave the *adhan* for the prayer. Then he quickly came down in a state of anger and woke them up for the prayer. One of the *fuqara* said to him, 'Sidi, the second *adhan* has not been called yet.' The Shaykh replied to him, 'That is the *adhan* for women. You must get up early. I will never allow you to be lax about the prayer while you are seekers of knowledge affiliated to the people of Allah.'

The noble Habibiyya *zawiya* was a mosque in which the prayer was regularly performed as well as being a school where people came to study and in which different types of knowledge were taught, and it was also a teaching centre for purification of the selves. It followed a precise programme. Activity began in it from before dawn. That was when the *fuqara* got up to pray *tahajjud* prayers until the *adhan* for *Subh*. After the *adhan*, the *jalala* refrain was repeated in a specific way. Then the Shaykh ﷺ came and led the people in the prayer, acting as imam. Then he ﷺ gave a brief lesson. After that the group went about their business. Those *fuqara* who were divested remained in the *zawiya* to perform the *wird*s and *dhikr*s which they were tasked with. Every Thursday night Sayyidina Shaykh ﷺ held a gathering of *dhikr* and discussion (*mudhākara*) and he ordered that that be kept up. He encouraged the *fuqara* to hold to the pure *shari'a* and to take on the Muhammadan character. Part of what he used to often repeat in this matter was: 'Whoever has no *adab* has no *tariq*'.

He ﷺ used to command people to have a good opinion of Allah and of His creatures, and to look at all of Allah's creation with the eye of esteem, to have love for the brothers in Allah Almighty, to gather for the sake of Allah and to be faithful to the *ba'ya*, and to do much *dhikr* of Allah Almighty, especially in the last third of the night. He ﷺ used to say, 'The station of *muraqaba* develops from much *dhikr* and then comes *mushahada*. When the heart of the servant is illuminated and the sun of his gnosis shines, he sees all of existence as blessing from Allah Almighty: the blessing of being brought into existence and the blessing of support which cannot be counted or numbered. Then he begins to love Allah Almighty by nature, intellect and *shari'a*.'

He ﷺ used to instruct his *muqaddams* to treat the *fuqara* well. That meant striving to give them good counsel, guiding them, asking about their circumstances, and being kind to them. Similarly, he instructed the *fuqara* to be good to their *muqaddams* by obeying them, respecting them, having love for them and showing good *adab* towards them. He insisted on holding to the community and avoiding division. Anyone who wants to learn the specifics of his teaching method only has to consult his noble *Diwan* which he called truly one of the treasures of spiritual instruction. In it he ﷺ compiled the quintessence of what the science of *tasawwuf* contains in this age.

When we are discussing his teaching method, we must point out that he ﷺ normally had a gathering every year a week after the Mawlid of the Chosen Beloved ﷺ to which many of the *fuqara* and lovers from both inside and outside Morocco would come. He would open the gathering by reciting a small amount of the Noble Qur'an and then the singers would begin singing and at a certain point the *fuqara* would stand for the *hadra* ('*imara*). When the *hadra* finished and the *fuqara* were seated, some clear *ayah*s of the Wise Book of Allah would be recited after which he ﷺ would give a discourse in which he explained the *ayah*s that had been recited. The gathering would end with supplication and then taking whatever hospitality (*ikramiyyat*) Allah had made feasible.

Our Shaykh 🌸 considered the *hadra* to be extremely important. He encouraged it and thought that it shortened the path of opening for the murid when they performed it with its preconditions. Some of his elite followers 🌸 reported to us that he 🌸 said, 'A *hadra* for a quarter of an hour is equal to a week's *khalwa*.' It is also related that he said, 'When three *fuqara* join together in a circle of *dhikr* and do not stand for the *hadra*, I consider them misers.' Something that supports these transmissions is what happened to him once[i] when he was at a *walima* (wedding feast) in which the *fuqara'* gathered. In the course of it there was a *hadra* in which all present experienced an ecstatic state. When the *hadra* was over, he was asked to write some of the *waridat* (gifts resulting from *dhikr*) which came in that night. So Allah inspired him to his middle *qasida* in *ta* which begins:

> In the tavern of the Presence (*hadra*) we drank a wine
> of the lights that totally dispelled the darkness.

In this *qasida* he stresses the excellence of the *hadra* and the necessity of submitting to its people. He said:

> Here are ones who have obliterated their selves
> and plumbed every depth in the oceans of love.
> So submit to them for what you see of their ardent love,
> and the dancing and singing in their dhikr of the Beloved.
> If you had but tasted something of the meaning of our words,
> you would have been one of the foremost in every circum-
> stance

---

i   One of those who related this event was Sidi al-Hajj at-Tahir Khallaf 🌸, the muqaddam of the Habibiyya in Mascara.

And, my brother you would have borne your troubles patiently,
and you would have rent the robes of shame and self-
importance.

You would have said to the leader of the people, "Make us love
His name!"

There is no shame in that song nor in that love!

Then he ﷺ warned against what happens if you deny it
or remain aloof from establishing it and he made it clear that
someone whose state is like this is controlled by his *nafs* and will
never be free of it, saying:

Unfortunately, whoever becomes subject to his own self
is cut off from the secrets of this Path.

His first hajj

Sidi Muhammad ibn al-Habib ﷺ decided in 1931 to travel to the
Holy Lands to perform the obligation of hajj, being sixty years
old at that time. It proved to be a very blessed time. He visited the
Rawda and when he was in front of the presence of his ancestor,
the Beloved Chosen One ﷺ, he composed his famous *qasida*:

'We are in present in the *Rawda* of the Messenger,
hoping for acceptance and welcome.'

After performing the rites of the hajj, he travelled to Syria and
met with its scholars, including Shaykh Tawfiq al-Ayyub and the
hadith scholar Badr ad-Din al-Hasani ad-Dimishqi,[i] may Allah

---

i Muhammad Badr ad-din al-Hasani, al-Maliki of school and ad-
Dimishqi (where he died). He was one of the great scholars and righteous men
of Damascus. He was born in Damascus in 1850 and died there in 1932.

have mercy on them both. Shaykh Badr ad-Din al-Hasani gave him an *ijaza* in writing. He had intended to meet with the one who loved the Messenger of Allah ﷺ and was his elegist, Sidi Yusuf an-Nabhani ﷺ, but he was told that he had gone to join the Highest Companion a few months before.[i]

He also went through the cities of Egypt and connected with a number of its scholars such as Shaykh Bakhit al-Muti'i[ii] and Shaykh Muhammad as-Samaluti,[iii] ﷺ. Our Shaykh made visits to those great scholars and engaged in a number of discussions. He was present in many scholarly and spiritual gatherings and they found him ﷺ to be an overflowing sea of gnosis, character and perfect *wilaya*. His splendid states dazzled them and they asked him to remain with them so that they could benefit from him, but he made his excuses to them. Then he returned to his land, making a detour to Algeria on the way, where he met with a group

---

i Sidi an-Nabhani died at the beginning of Ramadan 1350 or the beginning of January 1932. From this date, we can deduce that the first hajj of our Shaykh ﷺ was in 1932.

ii Muhammad Bakhit al-Muti'i al-Hanafi. He was born in Asyut, Egypt in 1854, He was the leading scholar of his age and imam of his time. He was eminent in the science of fundamental principles and deduction of legal judgements. He did not cease teaching traditional and erudite areas of knowledge of the *shari'a* to students seeking noble knowledge in every place he stayed. He taught lengthy books in the sciences of *tafsir, hadith, fiqh, usul al-fiqh, tawhid*, philosophy, logic and other things. He occupied the position of Mufti of Egypt from 1914 to 1920. He died in 1935 in Egypt.

iii Shaykh Ibrahim ibn 'Ali al-Hamidi as-Salamluti al-Azhari al-Maliki, a faqih and hadith scholar of al-Azhari and an Egyptian poet. He was born in the city of Salamlut (in the Governorate of Minya in Upper Egypt) in 1857 and died in Cairo in 1934.

of its scholars and righteous men. Many of them took the tariqa from him. They were the first core who spread the *Habibiyya Tariqa* in the regions of Algeria.

When he entered the town of Figuig in the southeast of Morocco, its scholars, led by Shaykh Muhammad, the Qadi ﷺ, received him. He found them engaged in reading *Sahih al-Bukhari* and they asked him to attend with them and he agreed to do that. He began his lessons with commentary on al-Bukhari from beginning to end. This was in addition to giving a commentary on the *Murshid al-Mu'in*. He remained in Figuig for nine months. That period was a reason for many of the inhabitants of Figuig and its regions joining his *tariqa*.

His second and third hajjs

His second journey to hajj was in 1360/1942. He ﷺ used to travel often in Morocco and Algeria to teach the pure Islamic *deen* and call people to the path of the people of Allah. He had many students. Those who loved him increased when they saw some of the secrets, lights and *barakat* that took place at his hand. During his lifetime and after his death his *zawiyas* spread throughout Morocco and Algeria and to different regions of the world. During his lifetime he had close to fifty *zawiyas* in Algeria. By the grace of Allah Almighty, his English students, under their Shaykh, Abdalqadir as-Sufi, established a number of *zawiyas* in South Africa, the USA, Mexico and European countries like Britain, Spain and Germany.

At the beginning of 1972, he – may Allah purify his secret – left Meknes to go on hajj for the third time accompanied by some of his *murids* and his wives[i] 🕮. He stopped in Blida in Algeria after falling ill and died from that illness 🕮 when he was a little over 100 years old. The date of his death 🕮 was Monday, 23 Dhu al-Qa'da 1391/11 January 1972. The words of Allah Almighty in the Wise Revelation apply to him: *'If anyone leaves his home, making hijra to Allah and His Messenger, and death catches up with him, it is Allah Who will reward him. Allah is Ever-Forgiving, Most Merciful.'* (4:100) As do the words of the Prophet 🕮 in the noble hadith: 'Whoever leaves in this way for hajj or *'umra* and dies in it will not be presented nor taken for reckoning. He will be told, "Enter the Garden."'[26] It has also come that the Prophet 🕮 said, 'Whoever leaves his house, intending the hajj, and dies before performing hajj, Allah Almighty will assign an angel to replace them in the hajj every year until the Day of Rising.'[27] In another hadith reported from Abu Hurayra 🕮 the Prophet 🕮 said, 'Whoever goes out for hajj or *'umra* or an expedition and then dies on the way, Allah will write for him the reward of a raider, or hajji or someone doing

---

i   Sayyidina Shaykh first married one of his relatives called Lalla Fatima. She used to hope that Allah would provide her with a child by him and she saw the Prophet 🕮 in a dream and he informed her that Sidi Muhammad ibn al-Habib would have no children. She died after an illness. Then our shaykh married the *sayyida*, Lalla al-Batul, and then divorced her. He later married the noble ladies: Lalla Fatima ad-Darqawi (she had the title Lalla Yatu) from the city of Midelt, Lalla Zhur from Taourirt in the Qsabi region, and Lalla Rabi'a Amami from the city of Tifelt, all of whom were Moroccan. The last of his wives, and the youngest of them, was the Algerian, Lalla Zulaykha, from Beni Tamou, commune of Abou al-Hassen, city of Chlef. She died in 2017 and is buried next to him. May Allah have mercy on all of them and make them abide in the Highest Paradise!

'umra until the Day of Rising.'[28] Praise be to Allah for these good tidings and the great blessing He gave to our Shaykh ﷺ and may He grant him a place in the Highest Paradise in the neighbourhood of his ancestor, the Beloved Chosen One ﷺ.

He was first buried in his *zawiya* in the town of Blida. He ﷺ himself instigated the excavation of his grave there a week before he died. Then nineteen days later he was moved to his *zawiya* in Meknes at the request of his family and murids. A radiant miracle (*karama*) occurred in the transport of his body witnessed by all those present. When his noble grave was opened, pure fragrant scent spread from it. All of those who were present there smelt it. They found his body unchanged, exactly as it had been when it was first placed there. He was reburied in his *zawiya* in Meknes at Derb al-Basha, near the Zitouna Mosque, after 'Asr on Monday, 14 Dhu al-Hijja, in the place where he had originally instructed that he should be buried. It is where his tomb now is.[29] May Allah purify his secret! The effulgence of his secrets continues to burst forth, moving through the world, from one nation to another, among his many sincere and righteous followers who travel on his straight path and convey it to others after them with trustworthiness love and truthfulness, without any change or alteration.

As for his books, to this day no prose works from his hand have reached us except for a long handwritten letter he sent to King Muhammad V ﷺ and some handwritten letters he sent to his students. There are also some audio tapes of his *tafsir* of some *ayah*s of *Surat al-A'raf* and *al-An'am* recorded in his *zawiya* in Meknes during the Ramadan of the last year of his life. He also left a world renowned *Diwan* containing some selections of his poetry and his *wird* which has been published a number of times in Morocco, Algeria and elsewhere. It is called: *Bughyat al-muridin as-sa'irin wa tuhfat as-salikin al-'Arifin* (The Desire of the Journeying Murids and the Gift to the Wayfaring Gnostics). In it he compiled a quintessence of his knowledge of the science of *tasawwuf* and the *qasidas* in it are sung at gatherings of his followers and, indeed, are now sung by many people of differing *tariqas* throughout the world.

This noble *Diwan* is considered to be a complete guide for those travelling the path of *tasawwuf,* instructing every *murid* who seeks to achieve the stations of Islam, *Iman* and *Ihsan.* It has been translated into English by some of his English students. The late scholar, Muhammad ibn al-Fatimi as-Sulami, known as Ibn al-Hajj, said, 'He wrote a commentary on the *Hafiza* of the noble Shaykh, Sidi Muhammad ibn al-'Arabi al-Madighri ﷺ in which he compiled some supplications of the Prophet ﷺ, Qur'anic *ayat*s, and some of the Shadhili *hizb*s, and also a commentary of the Mashishiyya prayer.'[30] However, as yet we have not been able to find these works. We ask Allah Almighty to give us success in discovering them and publishing them.

May Allah have mercy on this spiritual Qutb and purify his secret and honour him with a dwelling place in the Highest Paradise, and give us and all the Muslims the gift of following him and all the righteous *awliya'* of Allah, the heirs of the most noble Messenger and the most Beloved, our Beloved and the delight of our eyes, our Master Muhammad. May the best prayer and purest greeting be on him and on his family and Companions. Amin. Amin Amin. We end our supplication with: 'Praise be to Allah, the Lord of all the worlds.'

Endnotes

1. See Muhammad ibn Ja'far ibn Idris al-Kittani, *Salwa al-anfas wa muhaditha al-akyas*, edited by 'Abdullah al-Kamil al-Kittani and others, Dar ath-Thaqafa li'n-nashr wa'l-tawzi', Dar al-Bayda', Morocco, 2/245-247.

2. Shaykh Sidi Muhammad ibn Al-Habib, copy of a letter to Sultan Muhammad V, the King of Morocco, manuscript in the Habibiyya Zawiyya in Laghouat, Algeria.

3. Sidi Muhammad ibn al-Habib, copy of a manuscript of a letter to Sultan Muhammad V, p. 3.

4. Sidi Muhammad ibn Muhammad al-Qurashi, audio recording.

5. Sidi Muhammad ibn al-Habib, copy of a letter to Sultan Muhammad V.

6. Ibid.

7. Ibid.

8. Abu 'Abdullah Muhammad ibn 'Abdullah al-Kharashi al-Maliki, d. 1101 AH, the author of a commentary on the *Mukhtasar* of Khalil.

9. 'Ali ibn Mukarram Allah al-'Adawi as-Sa'idi, d. 1189 AH.

10. Abu Zakariyya Shared ad-din Yahya ar-Ruhuni, the Maliki *faqih* from Ruhuna, a tribe in the mountains of Ghunara in Morocco. He died in 773 AH.

11. See *Bulghat al-Arib fi akhbar Sidi Muhammad ibn al-Habib*, inside the *Diwan, Bughyat al-muridin as-sa'irin wa Tuhfat as-salikin al-'arifin*, published by Ibn Salim, Laghouat, p. 26, 2012.

12. He died in 1341/1923 and is buried in the quarter of al-Blida in Fes.

13. Shaykh Sidi Muhammad ibn al-Habib. *Bughyat al-muridin was tuhfat as-salikin al-'arifin*, compiled by Sidi 'Umar Abu Hafs, Algeria, 2nd edition, 1949, Foreword, p. 3.

14. Ibid.

15. Sidi Muhammad Belqurshi, ibid.

16. Sidi Muhammad ibn al-Habib, letter to Sultan Muhammad V, pp. 7-8.

17. <?> Ibid.

46

18. Shaykh Sidi Muhammad ibn al-Habib, *Diwan, Bughyat al-muridin as-sa'irin*, second edition, 1949, foreword, p. 5.

19. Ibid, p. 4.

20. Ibid, p. 4.

21. Ibid, pp. 3-4.

22. Sidi Muhammad ibn al-Habib, letter to Sultan Muhammad V, p.4.

23. Sidi Muhammad ibn al-Habib, letter to Sultan Muhammad V, p. 5.

24. Shaykh Ahmad ibn Mustafa al-'Alawi, *Dawhat al-asrar fi ma'na as-salat 'ala al-Mukhtar*, Mostaghanem, Algeria, third edition, 1991, p. 12.

25. Shaykh Sidi Muhammad ibn al-Habib, letter to Sultan Muhammad V, pp. 9-10.

26. Muhammad ibn al-Fatimi known as Ibn al-Hajj, *Is'af al-Ikhwan ar-raghibin bi-tarajim thullat min 'ulama' al-Maghrib al-Mu'asirin*, al-Jadid publishers, Morocco, 1992, p. 176.

27. Abu al-Fadl Muhammad ibn al-Mughayzal al-Maghribi ash-Shadhili, *al-Kawakib az-zahira fi ijtima' al-awliya' yaqazatan bi-Sayyid ad-Dunya wa'l-Akhira*, edited by Dr. Muhammad ibn Barika, Dar al-Fikr, Damascus, firs edition, 2011, p. 208.

28. Al-Bayhaqi, *Shu'ab al-Imam*, from Abu Hurayra, selection of *Kanz al-'Ummal*, 11847, 11848.

29. Muhammad ibn al-Fatimi known as Ibn al-Hajj, *Is'af al-Ikhwan ar-raghibin bi-tarajim thullat min 'ulama' al-Maghrib al-Mu'asirin*, al-Jadid publishers, 1992, p. 177.

30. *Is'af al-Ikhwan ar-raghibin*, p. 176.

Surat al-A'raf

7:156-180

1 al-A'raf 7:156-157

وَرَحْمَتِي وَسِعَتْ كُلَّ شَيْءٍ فَسَأَكْتُبُهَا لِلَّذِينَ يَتَّقُونَ وَيُؤْتُونَ الزَّكَوٰةَ وَالَّذِينَ هُم بِـَٔايَـٰتِنَا يُؤْمِنُونَ ۝ الَّذِينَ يَتَّبِعُونَ الرَّسُولَ النَّبِيَّ الْأُمِّيَّ الَّذِى يَجِدُونَهُۥ مَكْتُوبًا عِندَهُمْ فِى التَّوْرَىٰةِ وَالْإِنجِيلِ يَأْمُرُهُم بِالْمَعْرُوفِ وَيَنْهَىٰهُمْ عَنِ الْمُنكَرِ وَيُحِلُّ لَهُمُ الطَّيِّبَـٰتِ وَيُحَرِّمُ عَلَيْهِمُ الْخَبَـٰٓئِثَ وَيَضَعُ عَنْهُمْ إِصْرَهُمْ وَالْأَغْلَـٰلَ الَّتِى كَانَتْ عَلَيْهِمْ فَالَّذِينَ ءَامَنُوا بِهِۦ وَعَزَّرُوهُ وَنَصَرُوهُ وَاتَّبَعُوا النُّورَ الَّذِىٓ أُنزِلَ مَعَهُۥٓ أُولَـٰٓئِكَ هُمُ الْمُفْلِحُونَ ۝

My mercy extends to all things but I will prescribe it for those who have taqwa and pay zakat, and those who believe in Our Signs: those who follow the Messenger, the Unlettered Prophet, whom they find written down with them in the Torah and the Gospel, commanding them to do right and forbidding them to do wrong, making good things halal for them and bad things haram for them, relieving them of their heavy loads and the chains which were around them. Those who believe in him and honour him and help him, and follow the Light that has been sent down with him, they are the ones who are successful. (7:156-7)

Allah *subhanahu wa ta'ala* says in His Mighty Book: "*My Mercy embraces all things, and I shall prescribe it for those who have taqwa.*" We have started with this *surah* which we were talking about last year when we reached His words, *ta'ala*: *"And My Mercy embraces all things."* The name of this *surah* is *Surat al-A'raf*. Every *surah* gets its name from a word in it. So for example *Surat al-Baqara* is called *al-Baqara* because Allah mentions a cow in it. It is the same with *Al 'Imran* and with *an-Nisa'* and so on. The name of this *surah* is *al-A'raf* and Allah says in it: *"on the dividing wall* (al-a'raf) *are men."* Every *surah* gets its name from a word in it. It was revealed to the Prophet ﷺ in Makka al-Mukarrama.

Anyway, we reached Allah's words, *"And My Mercy extends to all things."* This mercy which embraces all things is a mercy without limit; but there is also a mercy which is restricted. This unlimited mercy encompasses animals, plants, angels, Prophets, Messengers, *awliya'*, and even the *mushrikun* and the *kafirun*. They all come within the scope of this mercy which entails existence and provision. Allah *ta'ala* gives everyone existence and sustains them. But then He makes them different in their beliefs. Among them are *muminun* and *kafirun* and *munafiqun*. But all of them share existence and sustenance.

This mercy even includes Iblis; even he shares in it. Once he was with one of the *'arifin* and he said, "I too claim a share in that mercy because Allah says: *'And My Mercy extends to all things,'* and I am a thing." The *'arif* said to him, 'But Allah has limited it by His Words: *'And I shall prescribe it for those who have taqwa.'"* He said to him, "You don't know anything," – this was Iblis talking to Sahl ibn Abdallah – "because how can something which Allah has made unlimited then have limits imposed on it?" This mercy without limit is of existence and sustenance. Everyone is included in it. The *kafirun* have existence and sustenance, so has Shaytan and so has everything else.

However, differentiation does exist, so what is it in? It's in *iman*. The people who follow the Prophets and Messengers and believe in them have a special place. They will be among the people of the Garden. They will enjoy the vision of the Noble Face of Allah. But the people who only have existence and sustenance without any *iman* will have their repayment in the Fire forever. They will be forever in the Fire. Because Allah then says: *"And I shall prescribe it,"* in other words that mercy; but prescribe it for whom? *"for those who have taqwa."* So the person who wants that prescribed, restricted mercy must have *taqwa*.

What is *taqwa*? It is obedience to all the commands of Allah and avoidance of all that is forbidden. The things that Allah has commanded us to do are the prayer, *zakat*, fasting, Hajj, and the things he has forbidden us are pride, envy, malice, hatred, bad thoughts about others. These people will taste that second kind of mercy because they have *taqwa*. *"And I shall prescribe it for those who have taqwa."* We have said that *taqwa* means to obey Allah's commands, and the person who has *taqwa* of Allah in this way will receive mercy. They will experience mercy in this existence, in their grave, at their rising, and in the *akhira*. But all those who do not have *taqwa* will be in misery. They will be punished in this existence, in their grave, in the *akhira*, in everything of theirs. *Taqwa* gains for you every good quality.

He says, *ta'ala*: *"And I shall prescribe it for those who have taqwa."* Sidi Ibn 'Ashir says:

The attainment of *taqwa* is by avoidance
and obedience, inward and outward.

Thus you obtain it.
It has four divisions for the traveller
on the path of profit.
He lowers his eyes to what is forbidden
and restrains his ears from evil.
He guards his private parts
and fears the Witness.
He delays matters until he knows
what Allah has decreed for him in them.

If you want to do something you should ask about it first. Allah says: *"Ask the people of the Remembrance if you do not know."* (16:43) No action is left to our own intellects. Not eating or drinking or clothing or anything else. The whole business refers back to what? To the Muhammadan *shari'a*: *"Whatever the Messenger gives you you should accept and whatever he forbids you you should forgo."*

Then we also have *taqwa* against *shirk*. *Shirk* is the subject of much discussion by the *'ulama'* of this time and they ascribe it to people. We divide *shirk* into two types: open *shirk* and hidden *shirk*. To avoid open *shirk*: a man must know the attributes of *Mawlana subhanah*, because if someone does not know Allah he cannot truly affirm His unity. Sidi ibn 'Ashir says:

The first duty of the one under obligation
who has been given sanity
Is to know Allah and His Messenger
by the attributes which the *ayahs* make clear.

If people know Allah by His attributes they won't go wrong. They will know the vastness of the attributes of *Mawlana* and that no one has any share in them, neither Prophet nor angel nor *wali* nor Messenger. If people don't know Allah, they cannot help but be destroyed. They say, "Sayyidina Muhammad cured you," or "so and so helped me," and so on. But if someone truly knows Allah – that effective power belongs to Him, specified will belongs to Him, absolute knowledge belongs to Him, particularised wisdom belongs to Him – if they know Allah in this way they will not be destroyed. If they know Allah they will never, for example, associate Him with an angel or a *wali* or a Prophet or a Messenger. All the *'ulama'* are agreed about this: that our first obligation is to know Allah by His attributes.

And what are His attributes? There are the attributes of the Essence of Allah – the *salbiyya* attributes, the *ma'ani* attributes, and the *ma'nawiyya* attributes. There are twenty attributes that everyone should know. The first attribute is existence. *Mawlana* has the attribute of existence, but his existence isn't like our existence. His existence is from before time. He has no beginning. Before time, no beginning. And His existence is obligatory.

We divide obligations into two: obligations of the *shari'a* and obligations of the intellect. The obligations of the *shari'a* are those things for whose performance you are rewarded and for whose abandonment you are punished. The obligations of the intellect are those things whose non-existence cannot be conceived. This existence of *Mawlana* is an obligation of the intellect. His non-existence cannot be conceived, because He is from before time and goes on forever. Before time and going on forever. If the obligatory nature of His before-timeness is in your intellect and the obligatory nature of His going-on-forever is in your intellect, you will never make His existence conditional. His existence is obligatory on Him. There is no beginning to His existence and no end to His existence. He has Before-timeness and Going-on-without-end. These two attributes apply to the Essence of Allah *ta'ala*.

So there are the *salbiyya* attributes. They are Before-timeness, Going-on-forever, Unaffectedness-by-events, and Oneness of Essence, Attributes and Actions. They do not take anything away from Allah rather they take away from our intellects everything that cannot be applied to Allah. If we know that Allah is Before-time we cannot form a picture in our intellects of His coming into being in time, and if we know He is Going-on-forever we cannot conceive of His annihilation. Likewise, if we recognise that He has unlimited wealth it is impossible for us to imagine Him ever being in need. And so on ... If we recognise that He is not affected by events we know that nothing can be the same as Him, not in His essence, not in His attributes and not in His actions. This is the first thing a person should know. Sidi ibn 'Ashir says about this:

The first duty of the one under obligation
    who has intellect
Is to know Allah and His Messenger
    by the attributes upon which the *ayahs* make clear.

This is where the Wahhabis and others like them go wrong when they say, "You people don't know Allah. You are committing *shirk?*" But if someone knows Allah in this way they cannot make any mistake. They will never confuse Allah with anything else. *Sidi Mawlana* has necessary attributes. Before-timeness to which there is no beginning. Not equal to Him is any Prophet or Messenger or *wali* or angel. *"Nothing is like Him. He is the All-Hearing, the All-Seeing."* (42:11) *"And no one is comparable to Him."* (112:4)

He has no equal, not in His Essence nor His Attributes nor His Actions. If someone knows their Lord in this way they just can't go wrong. They know that nothing can be similar to Him. It is Him we serve as slaves, Him we prostrate to, Him we bow to, and Him we glorify. The whole creation is variegated into many layers. Everything has its own degree. There are the degrees of the angels, the degrees of the Prophets, the degrees of the Messengers, the degrees of the *awliya'*. Everyone has their own degree. But everyone is a slave to Allah. *"There is no one in the heavens and the earth who will not come to the All-Merciful as a slave."* All of us are slaves to *Sidi Mawlana*.

"Those who have taqwa," against *shirk* – open and hidden. We have been talking about open *shirk*. But hidden shirk is very common in people. Such as when someone says, "It was so and so who benefitted me," or "that medicine which I took was what cured me of that illness." What's that called? That is hidden *shirk*. Someone says, "It was so and so who did that thing for me," or "This clothing is what gave me warmth, if it wasn't for it I would have died of the cold." Or again, "That drink I had was what quenched my thirst." This giving intrinsic reality to the means is known as hidden *shirk*, but only if you attribute effective power to it, not of course if you know that Allah alone is the real cause of things when they happen.

You would then say that the clothing was the means to my getting warm, or this food was the means by which my hunger was satisfied but it was Allah alone who made it happen. It is always necessary for there to be a means. "Means must always exist and an unseen cause behind them." But most of the time people go wrong. They say, "If it wasn't for so and so I would never have achieved my aim." What do you mean? It is Allah who gives it to you. As He says: *"It is He Who has made everything in the heavens and everything on the earth subservient to you. Directly from Him."* (45:13)

However, you must thank the means. Really! Thank the person at whose hands you receive a good thing; thank them either by some good action or by making a *du'a*. It is said: "If someone has done you a good service, repay them, and if you cannot then pray for them until you think they have been repaid." You should say, "Such a one has helped me and been the means to good things for me. *Ya Rabbi*, take his hand. *Ya Rabbi*, give him expansion. *Ya Rabbi*, protect him and his children." This we must do; but at the same time we mustn't forget that it is in reality Allah alone who benefits us. He subjected the other person to us and He turned his heart towards us so that the good thing reached us. But if we ascribe the whole thing to the creature that becomes hidden *shirk*. Allah says: *"Most of them do not believe in Allah without being mushrikun."* (12:106)

Try to understand this. Those who affirm Allah's Unity must do so inwardly and outwardly. The means have no innate effectiveness, not even if the means is a Prophet or a *wali* or an angel or a Messenger. Allah made them a means for us. If it wasn't for the Prophet ﷺ we would not know Allah. He is Allah's means to our happiness. We will all, *insha'a'llah*, be among the people of the Garden through following him. These things are all means, but Allah *ta'ala* is the Doer in every instance. There is no Doer but Allah. Allah made these means His instruments and we must show correct behaviour towards them. You should not let there be a case of anyone doing something for you, or giving you something, without your thanking them for it. If you have something to repay them with, then give it to them, and if not, then pray for them till you think you've fulfilled your obligation towards them. But if you hold them to be the effective cause – believe that it was really them that caused whatever it was to be given to you, that they did it by their own power – then this is *shirk;* and, if you're not careful, it might even turn out to be open rather than hidden *shirk.*

Allah says: *"Those who have taqwa."* We have been explaining to you the meaning of *taqwa.* Allah says in His Mighty Book, talking of its benefits: *"Have taqwa of Allah and He will give you knowledge."* (2:282) *"Allah only accepts from those who have taqwa."* (5:27) *"Those who have taqwa will be amid Gardens and Rivers on seats of honour in the presence of an all-powerful King."* (54:54-5) So you see, *taqwa* is the means to all good both in this world and the Next. If you have *taqwa* of Allah He will make your provision easy to obtain, you will be loved by His slaves, and your life will be made easy for you here and in the *akhira.* When you go to the grave you will find it comfortable, and when you go to the Place of Rising you will find the same. On the other hand, if you have no *taqwa* you will be in misery both in this world and the Next. *Taqwa* is what gathers together all good. Allah tells us that He will provide for those who have *taqwa.* So the thing people really need more than anything else is *taqwa.* And if you have *taqwa* of Allah you will carry out His commands and avoid what He has forbidden and keep company with the people of blessings.

But remember that no one can get anything except through specific means. And as for those people who say that the means are unnecessary – where would they get knowledge from if there wasn't an *'alim* to teach them? How could they know anything? You must affirm the means. "It is necessary to have the means accompanied by wisdom." But watch out that you don't give those means innate effectiveness and say, for instance, that if it wasn't for so and so I would never have attained that thing. No! So and so is only the means and it is Allah who is the Doer and Designer. But also watch out that you don't deny the means and say that people have no part in it. This is a serious mistake. Why is that? Because it's *haqiqa* without *shari'a*. The *shari'a* makes things clear for us and gives everything its due. The Prophet ﷺ says to us, "If someone does you a good turn..." and he is that created being who is the means to our Islam, he says to us, "If someone does you a good turn, repay him." Know that they are the means to the good thing you received. All this that I've been saying has been about the *ayat*: *"My mercy encompasses all things and I will prescribe it for those who have taqwa."*

and pay the zakat.

Zakat is what people today disregard almost completely and in this they go very badly wrong. They say, "These taxes and rates we pay take the place of *zakat*." But that is not the case. *Zakat* is to take care of those who are weak and poor, and these people still exist. Allah says: *"Zakat is for the poor and the destitute..."* (9:60) The taxes you pay are to support the administration so that they can look after you and ensure your safety, so that you can rest tranquil in your houses. If there wasn't any support for the administration we would live in chaos. We need people to guard us and to watch over the roads and these things require financing, and where does the money to do that come from? From the people. But we can't say it takes the place of *zakat*.

This support of the administration and the taxes which go towards it are so that the whole business can be kept going. We could never do all this by ourselves. If there was no administration we would not be able to manage. The administration is over us from us. This gathering of ours is to their credit. If there was no security you couldn't come and I wouldn't see you. Allah says: *"So let them worship the Lord of this House who has preserved them from hunger and secured them from fear."* There has to be a means to this "securing from fear", there must be a functioning administration which employs people to guard us and to watch over the roads so that people can travel in safety and so that people who want to come can do so in security, and so that people can sleep safely in their houses. We mustn't begrudge the administration anything we give them and we must realise that what we give is to meet the cost of our security, to pay those who work towards it. But *zakat*, no, that is exclusively to look after the poor and destitute. Look out for the weak and destitute and take care of them. Give to them until you have paid what is due from you.

"Those who have taqwa and pay the zakat and those who believe in our ayats." The ayats of *Sidi Mawlana* are many. He shows them to us through the revealed Books. Which Books are the ones we believe in? The Torah, the Injil, the Psalms and the Furqan, and we also believe in in the angels and in all those things that are hidden from us, the things of the *akhira* such as the Rising, the *Sirat*, the Balance, the Basin, the Garden with its ascending degrees and the Fire with its descending degrees.

those who believe in our signs: those who follow the Messenger.

Now the Bani Isra'il asked for instructions during the time of Sayyidina Musa and Allah gave them what they asked for but they didn't accept them and so He gave them to us, the Muhammadan community, instead. He said to them, "I give you the whole earth to pray in wherever you go and I authorise you to recite your Torah without using the book." They said, "We will only pray in a synagogue – knowing quite well what Allah had told them – and we won't recite the Torah except from scrolls." Allah has made the whole earth pure for us to pray in. This is what Allah has given us. We don't have to look for a mosque when we want to do the prayer. No matter where we are when the time of prayer comes, we can do the prayer there. But as for them, this is veiled from them and they will only pray in their synagogues. *Mawlana* gave them a choice in this matter and they chose the synagogue. And they also chose not to recite their Torah by heart like we recite the Qur'an. Allah made the Qur'an easy for us. We can recite by heart. Some recite by heart and others with the Book. This is veiled from them; they can only recite if they have the Torah in their hands. This just goes to show. Allah gave all the easy things to Bani Israil and they didn't accept them. When they refused to accept them who did Allah give them to? To this Muhammadan community.

Those who follow the Messenger, the unlettered Prophet, whom they find written down with them in the Torah and the Injil.

A complete description of Sayyidina Muhammad is written down in the Torah and his description is also in the Injil, but the enemies of Allah changed and altered the Injil and changed and altered the

Torah. This was so that those in power among them and their *'ulama* – or those they call *'ulama* – could deceive the majority of the people and keep them under their control. The Torah and the Injil both had descriptions of Sayyidina Muḥammad ﷺ and of this Muhammadan community, but as we said, the enemies of Allah changed and altered them.

commanding them to do right, forbidding them from doing wrong, making good things halal for them

Right is the best of what is in the *shari'a* and wrong is what is opposed to the *shari'a*. The things that are good have been made halal for us and other things have been forbidden like wine and smoking and other things that have a bad smell. The believer is required to give these things up and if it isn't in his power to do so and he can't find a cure, he should begin to cut down on them and take them like a medicine. Because there are people who are advised against doing something and then they just don't know how they can do anything about it.

There was a *sharif* with me on hajj who used to smoke, poor man. I said to him, "Now you've performed hajj and visited the Prophet ﷺ, give this up." So he stopped smoking. Then we went to get the bus back to Jeddah and he nearly got into a fight with the driver. I saw that his eyes were red and that he was completely out of control, so I said to him, "Go and take that medicine of yours! But reduce the amount and make the intention to only use it as a medicine." If Allah helps someone and they manage to give the thing up in one go then that of course is the best thing, but if they know they won't be able to, they should take less of it and be aware that they are only doing it to cure themselves of their habit. This so that you can put your house in order and so that everything doesn't go sour on you. However, if someone just indulges his appetite, doing it again and again, then that can be a real disaster for him.

and bad things haram for them, relieving them of their heavy loads and the chains which were around them.

In the Bani Israil if a man committed a wrong action he would be told, "Go and kill yourself." Or, "Go and wander in the desert until you die." Or, "Burn all your clothes." Their affairs and their *tawba* entailed great suffering. As for us, Allah has lifted that suffering from us. If a man commits a wrong action, then makes *tawba* to *Sidi Rabbi*, asks for forgiveness, Allah accepts his *tawba*. He tells us: *"It is He Who accepts tawba from His slaves and pardons their wrong action and knows what they do."* (42:25) In any case, the Prophet ﷺ said, *"Tawba erases everything that came before it."* It wipes out everything. It removes every single one of your wrong actions. But with Bani Israil it was otherwise. Their *tawba* wasn't like this. Allah told them: "Go and wander till you die." Or, "Kill yourself." Their *tawba* was very difficult. Allah *ta'ala* lifted this hardship from us.

Those who believe in him and honour him.

There are people who don't honour him ﷺ and they are wrong not to because Allah has ordered us to honour what He has honoured. Allah says about Sayyidina Muhammad ﷺ: *"Those who pledge you their allegiance, pledge allegiance to Allah."* (48:10) And He says: *"Whoever obeys the Messenger has obeyed Allah."* (4:80) Allah has ordered us to honour what He has honoured and we do so to fulfil His command. The exaltedness of his degree ﷺ is such that no-one can hope to attain it. Sayyidina Muhammad ﷺ, it is by his hand that Allah has shown mercy to this community; it is through him that we are able to know Allah and enter the Garden and enjoy the vision of the Noble Face of Allah. All of this is through Sayyidina Muhammad ﷺ. We don't forget the gift of Sayyidina Muhammad and it is for this reason that Allah has ordered us to pray for blessings on him. We pray so that we can repay a little of what we owe him. He is the means to our happiness and our entering the Garden and our enjoyment of the vision of the Noble Face of Allah. *"And honour him and help him,"* against his enemies.

And follow the light that has been sent down with him.

What is the light that was sent down with him ﷺ? It is the Qur'an. What is this light that was sent down with Sayyidina Muhammad ﷺ? It is the Qur'an. This Qur'an, in it Allah has gathered together everything. In it is the meaning of the Torah, the meaning of the Injil, the meaning of the Psalms and every other matter. Allah has gathered everything together in it for us. There's only one thing we need to focus our hearts on – and what's that? The Book of Allah! And on the Sunna which makes it clear! Allah *ta'ala* made the Qur'an an encircling ocean but in it there are certain things to which we have no immediate access. The Sunna came and made clear to us the things in the Book of Allah that were difficult to understand. Then after that the right-acting *'ulama* came and they too elucidated for us things which were not clear. In any case the Book and the Sunna are the path which leads to happiness but the only one who can know this is the one who knows its people.

The ordinary man who spends all day in idle pastimes, wasting his days – if he wants to learn about the Book and the Sunna he must look for the people of Allah, who are those who will teach him how to do the prayer and how to do *wudu'* and how to know Allah. If he does this he will undoubtedly gain a great gift. But if, for example, he just stays in his every day occupations he will go to the mosque without any knowledge. A hadith tells us: "Allah cannot be worshipped except with knowledge." And another: "Seeking knowledge is an obligation on every Muslim man and woman." It is the duty of every husband to teach his wife how to do *wudu* and *ghusl* and how to do everything she is required to do. What she should do where her periods are concerned. The responsibility for her is on his shoulders. As the Prophet ﷺ said, "All of you are shepherds and all of you will be questioned about your flock." A man should ask his children whether they've done the prayer or not? When they come in from school, ask them, "Did you do the prayer there?" If they reply, "No, we didn't," tell them, "You know tomorrow on the Day of Rising you will be asked about the prayer." If they find their father insisting day after day about the prayer it's inevitable that they will do it. But if they come in and no one asks them they will not do the prayer.

Now in our time there's great laxity. We need teachers who encourage and fathers who are firm with their children. If teachers encourage their pupils to pray and fathers ask their children when they come home, "Have you prayed or not?" they will undoubtedly be aware of their *deen* and undoubtedly do the prayer. But if, for instance, a teacher prays but doesn't tell his pupils to and similarly a father doesn't ask his children, they will grow up without a scrap of the *deen* and will never do the prayer.

and follow the light that has been sent down with him, those, those are the ones who are successful.

They are the successful – those who follow Sayyidina Muhammad ﷺ and follow what he brought – the Book and the Sunna – they are the ones who will reap the harvest both in this world and the *akhira*. This is as far as we will go today, and tomorrow, *insha'allah*, we will continue.

al-A'raf 7:158

قُل يَـٰٓأَيُّهَا ٱلنَّاسُ إِنِّى رَسُولُ ٱللَّهِ إِلَيْكُمْ جَمِيعًا ٱلَّذِى لَهُ
مُلْكُ ٱلسَّمَـٰوَٰتِ وَٱلْأَرْضِ لَآ إِلَـٰهَ إِلَّا هُوَ يُحْىِۦ وَيُمِيتُ فَـَٔامِنُوا۟
بِٱللَّهِ وَرَسُولِهِ ٱلنَّبِىِّ ٱلْأُمِّىِّ ٱلَّذِى يُؤْمِنُ بِٱللَّهِ وَكَلِمَـٰتِهِۦ وَٱتَّبِعُوهُ
لَعَلَّكُمْ تَهْتَدُونَ ۝

*Say: 'Mankind! I am the Messenger of Allah to you all,
of Him to Whom the kingdom of the heavens and the earth
belongs. There is no god but Him. He gives life and causes to
die. 'So have iman in Allah and His Messenger, the Unlettered
Prophet, who has iman in Allah and His words, and follow
him so that hopefully you will be guided.' (7:158)*

Allah *ta'ala* says in His Noble book: "*Say: 'O Mankind, I am
the Messenger of Allah to you all...*'" We have already mentioned
that this *surah* is named *Suratu'l-A'raf*. It is called *Suratu'l-A'raf*
because every *surah* is named after a word in it and in it Allah says:
"*On the A'raf there will be men...*" (7:46) So for that reason it is
called *Suratu'l-A'raf*. Anyway we reached where Allah says: "*Say:
'O Mankind...*'" This "*Say*" is a verb in the imperative tense and
it is an address from Allah to His Prophet ﷺ. Allah says to him:

"*Say: 'O mankind...'*" And what can be understood from His statement "*O mankind...*" is that the sending of the Prophet was to the whole of mankind. He didn't say "O tribe of Quraysh" or "O Arabs". No, He says: "*O mankind*" and the word "mankind" entails every community, whether they are Christians or Jews or Fire-worshippers, all of them. And anyone who doesn't believe in Sayyidina Muhammad 🙵 and dies in that state, dies as a *kafir*. Even if, according to his own understanding, his worship is correct. If he's following Sayyidina 'Isa or Sayyidina Musa or anyone else, that won't be of any benefit to him, because the *shari'a* of Sayyidina Muhammad abrogates all other *shari'as*.

For this reason Allah says: "*O Mankind, I am the Messenger of Allah to you all*" and the business of the Messenger is to deliver the Message and the Message is a transmission between Allah and His slaves in order that the evidence for or against them can be established. Allah says: "*We never punish until We have sent a Messenger.*" (17:15) There is no question of punishment until a Messenger has been sent to a people and he has made clear to them *Islam, Iman, Ihsan* and their *shari'a*, so that the evidence is there. Then if they follow that a state of happiness will be their's, and they will enter the Garden, but if they go against it they will be miserable and enter the Fire. It so that evidence for them or against them will be established.

Allah says: "*O Mankind, I am the Messenger of Allah to you...*" As we have said the Messenger is the one who conveys a Message from Allah – a human being who has a *shari'a* revealed to him and who is commanded to communicate it to his people. And he 🙵 did convey it and make it clear. And he didn't die until he had made clear to them everything that would bring them closer to Allah and had made clear to them everything that would distance them from Allah. He said in the *Khutba al-Wad'a*, "Is it not true that I have conveyed it?" They replied, "You have conveyed it, Messenger of Allah, and made it clear." And so the evidence was established for and against the whole of mankind, not just the Muslims. It doesn't matter whether people are Jews or Christians or Fire-worshippers. Anyone who doesn't believe in Sayyidina Muhammad ﷺ and dies in that state, dies as a *kafir*. Their actions do not benefit them nor does their belief in their Messenger. Anyway, Allah says: "*O Mankind, I am the Messenger of Allah to you all.*"

of Him to Whom the kingdom of the heavens and earth belongs,

Now we come to the description of Allah, *tabaraka wa ta'ala*. It is as if He were saying, "This One who is doing the sending, who is He?" Allah says describing Himself: "*Him to whom the kingdom of the heavens and earth belongs*" So He is the King, *subhanah*, and everything apart from Him is a slave to Him: "*There is no one in the heavens and earth who will not come to the All-Merciful as a slave.*" (19:93) Everyone is the slave of *Sidi Mawlana*, whether they are Messengers, Prophets, angels, human beings or jinn. Allah says: "*of Him to Whom the kingdom of the heavens and earth belongs*"

There is no god but Him

"*There is no god but Him*", "*There is no god but Him*". This "*no*" is the particle of negation. "*There is no god*" in other words, nothing can be rightly worshipped except who? Except Him *subhanah*. Every other object of worship is worthless. Anyone who worships anything other than Allah is a *kafir*. And if they die doing that they will be eternally in the Fire. As He tells us in *Surah an-Nisa'*: *"Allah does not forgive anything being associated with Him, but He forgives whoever He wills for other than that."* (4:48) He says: *"Him to whom the kingdom of the heavens and earth belongs. There is no god but Him."* This *"There is no god but Him."* What does it mean? That nothing can be rightly worshipped except Allah. Because the word "god" in Arabic means "object of worship". And we negate every object of worship – they are all worthless – except for our Lord, *subhanah.* He is rightly worshipped. Nothing is rightly worshipped except Allah.

And there is no doubt that this object of worship that we say is rightly worshipped, has attributes and it is obligatory for human beings to know what they are. What! Are you going to say "Allah" and do the prayer when you don't know who Allah is? What does Ibn 'Ashir say: "The first thing that is incumbent upon the legally capable person – as long as he is capable of reflection – is to know Allah and the Messengers by their attributes and qualities as they are made clear in the *ayahs.*" Nowadays people go wrong about this. In the past we used to know that when someone reached puberty the first thing they had to do was find out about *tawhid,* so that they would know the attributes of our Lord. The attributes that are necessary for Allah, those that are impossible for Him and those that are possible for Him. So that they then will know the meaning of "there is no god but Allah". Nowadays people say, "I've reached puberty" but they don't know the things they're supposed to know connected with it.

"There is no god..." Theologians, such as as-Sanusi and those who preceded him, made a statement that contains within it all the articles of faith. They said that the meaning of "there is no

god but Allah" is: nothing is independent of everything else and everything else is dependent on it, except Allah. He is rich beyond the need of anything else. He tells us: *"Allah is rich beyond need and you are the poor and in need."* (47:38) So He, *subhanah*, is wealthy beyond need of anything else and we, all of us, are poor and in need of Him, whether angel or Prophet or Messenger, all are poor and in need of Allah, *tabaraka wa ta'ala*. And through this we know that our Lord has existence, absolute existence, that is necessary in respect of Him. As for us, our existence is metaphorical, meaning that we are exposed to contingent events all the time; no one knows about themselves if they're going to stay well or die. But Allah's existence is necessary; His non-existence is inconceivable.

And He has eternal pre-existence and everlasting continuance. He is pre-eternally existent without beginning, everlastingly continuing without end. Absolutely independent and totally different from all created things. He says in His Book: *"Nothing is like Him, He is the All-Hearing, the All-Seeing."* (42:11) We have to know *Sidi Mawlana*; if we know Him we won't go wrong. Then we're not going to equate Him with an angel or Prophet or Messenger. These attributes of our Lord are far removed from anything that can be compared to created things. Allah says: *"Nothing is like Him..."* (112:4) In other words there is no resemblance whatsoever; not in its essence, nor its attributes, nor its actions.

If only these people who are responsible for today's youth would teach them about Allah; teach them what is necessary for Allah, what impossible for Him and what is possible for Him. If the slave knows his Lord he's not going to go wrong. He will know what a Prophet is and his rank, and an angel, and a Messenger and a *kafir*. He will know that our Lord, *subhanah*, has absolute independence and is above and beyond the attributes of created things. He has, *subhanah*, necessary existence. He has eternal pre-existence. What's the meaning of eternal pre-existence? It means He has no beginning. And what's the meaning of everlasting continuance? It means He has no end. And He has absolute wealth, we're all agreed that His wealth is absolute. He doesn't need to eat; He doesn't need to drink; He doesn't need to sleep. He has no need of anything at all. Because He's wealthy beyond need of anything else whatsoever. And He has Power, and Will and Knowledge and Life and Hearing and Sight and Speech. And He, *subhanah*, is Powerful, Willing, Knowing, Living, Hearing, Seeing and Speaking.

It's obligatory for every human being to know these attributes. And as long as they know that our Lord is not like any created thing, they won't go wrong. They will know what the rank of a Prophet or Messenger is and give them the high respect that is due to them. They will also know what an angel is, and a *wali*, for example, and a believer. But if they don't know Allah they'll go wrong. They'll get a *wali*, or something else, mixed up with the Divine. Whereas Allah says: *"Nothing is like Him…"*. If they know Allah they'll know that He transcends the attributes of all created things.

He has effective Power, His Power is effective in every instance, related to every possibility, every single possibility. And He has Will specifying every possibility. And He has Knowledge that encompasses every necessary, possible and impossible thing. And He has Sight encompassing every existent thing. And in this way human beings have to know these attributes of our Lord. And if they know them, they will know the meaning of "there is no god but Allah". "Nothing is independent of everything else and everything else is dependent on it, except Allah." Everything is in need of Allah, no matter whether they are angels or Prophets or Messengers – everything. Allah is absolutely independent of everything. If people know this they can't go wrong.

These things we are talking about are obligatory for us. And what does being obligatory mean? As we have already mentioned there are two kinds of obligation: legal obligations and intellectual obligations. Something is an intellectual obligation if its non-existence is inconceivable. A legal obligation is something, the performance of which results in reward and the abandonment of which results in punishment. You have to differentiate between legal obligations and intellectual obligations. For instance, in terms of legal obligations we say that the prayer is obligatory. What does it's being obligatory mean. It means that, if we don't do it, at some point we're going to be punished. Because, as we said, a legal obligation is something, the performance of which results in reward, and the abandonment of which results in punishment. That applies to the prayer, *zakat*, fasting and hajj. All these things that Allah has made obligatory for us, we are under obligation to carry them out. These are obligatory on account of being legal obligations. Things the performance of which results in reward, and the abandonment of which results in punishment.

Intellectual obligations aren't like that. They are matters whose non-existence is inconceivable. So we say that our Lord's existence is an intellectual obligation. That means it's something whose non-existence is inconceivable. And to know that He has power is an intellectual obligation. The non-existence of it is inconceivable.

And so on. That's the difference between an intellectual obligation and a legal obligation. And it's necessary for people to differentiate between things that are obligatory intellectually and things that are obligatory legally. Allah says: *"Say: 'Mankind, I am the Messenger of Allah to you all, of Him to whom the Kingdom of the heavens and earth belongs. There is no god but Him.'"*

He gives life and causes to die

"He gives life and causes to die." He gives life to whoever He wills and causes whoever He wills to die. Everything is based on the Divine Will. He says: *"You will not will unless Allah wills."* (76:30) All matters are subject to the Divine Will. Anyone who dies, does so by Allah's Will, or becomes poor, it is by Allah's Will, or becomes a *kafir*, it is by Allah's Will, or becomes Muslim, it is by Allah's Will; all of it goes back to the Divine Will. And the two words for will – *mashi'a,* and *irada* – mean the same thing. They have the same meaning. By it Allah specifies what He wills at exactly the time He wills. So we can say that this gathering of ours was preordained in Allah's Knowledge and that there was a specific time when it was going to happen, this time. This time in which Allah has gathered us together, is entirely dependent on the Divine Will. His Will specifies the things that are dependent on it. So this gathering was directly specified by this Divine Attribute to happen exactly as it has. It was preordained by the Knowledge of Allah, specified by His Will, brought out by His Power, put in place by His Wisdom. There is nothing in existence that has not been pre-ordained by His Knowledge, specified by His Will, brought out by His Power and put in place by His Wisdom.

So people must know these attributes. They govern everything in existence, whether heavenly or earthly, whether in the Garden or the Fire. There is nothing in existence that is not pre-ordained by Allah's Knowledge; and His Knowledge is from pre-eternity; it has no beginning. The whole affair is pre-ordained by His Knowledge from before time. Everything in existence is pre-ordained by His Knowledge and specified by His Will at a particular time; every single thing is brought about by His Will at the exact time specified for it. He has Power, He has Will and He has Knowledge. Everything is preordained by His Knowledge, specified by His Will, brought out by His Power, put in place by His Wisdom. These attributes belong to Him. He has Knowledge; He has Will; He has Power; and He has Wisdom. There is nothing in this creation that is not preordained by His Knowledge, specified by His Will, brought out by His Power, put in place by His Wisdom. He says in *Surah an-Naml*: *"The handiwork of Allah who creates everything with great precision."* (27:88)

"He gives life and causes to die…" There's no one who can give life to the living or cause the dead to die except our Lord, *subhanah*. No one else is capable of doing that. Our Lord is the one who gives life to whoever He wills and causes the death of whoever He wills. *"He gives life and causes to die"*.

So believe in Allah and His Messenger

Once we know that this Messenger ﷺ was commanded to convey the Message, what then becomes obligatory on us: belief in him! Allah says: *"So believe…"* What does *"believe"* mean here? It means affirm the truth, affirm the truth of this Messenger. Because that is what belief is: affirmation of the truth of something. It is to affirm the truth of what this Messenger has brought from Allah and to act on what he has commanded you to do and avoid what he has forbidden you to do. Allah says: "*Whatever the Messenger gives you you should accept and whatever he forbids you you should forgo. Have taqwa of Allah.*" (59:7)

Allah says: "*So believe in Allah…*" Belief entails affirmation with the heart, articulation with the tongue and action with the limbs. A human being is not a real believer until he affirms the existence of Allah with his heart, and the Attributes that belong to Him and the existence of the angels and the Resurrection and the *Sirat* and the Balance and the Basin and the Garden and the Fire. It's essential for every believer to affirm all those things with his heart, to know for certain that he's going to see all these things on the Last Day. The only thing separating him from them is his inevitable journey to the Next World. Then he'll see them all, the Balance, the *Sirat*, the Basin, the Garden and the Fire; the only thing between us and them is our departure from this world. It's necessary for every human being to believe in all these things, to believe in Allah and His Names and Attributes and His angels, and His Books, and His Messengers and the Last Day and everything connected to it. This has all come from His Words: '*So believe in Allah and His Messenger*'.

the unlettered Prophet

"*The unlettered Prophet…*" This is one of his miracles ﷺ. As is said: "His being unlettered and having this vast knowledge would be enough of a miracle on its own without the need for any other." This Prophet did not read and did not write nor go to any school nor did he meet any scholars. Allah *ta'ala* imbued him with all these knowledges and gnoses, and knowledge overflowed from him, knowledge of the spiritual Path, knowledge of the hidden realities and knowledge of the outward law. Allah says: *"and He taught you what you did not know before. Allah's favour to you is indeed immense.'* (4:113) Allah Himself taught him 🕌, not any human teacher, and Sayyidina Jibreel was the means by which that knowledge was conveyed. He was the one who conveyed the Qur'an to him. And, in this month of Ramadan, he used to revise it with him, go over it with him.

Anyway, as we said, we have to believe in Sayyidina Muhammad 🕌 and believe in everything he came with. And this belief can't just be with the tongue, just saying you believe in it. No, that's not belief; belief is affirmation with the heart. To the extent that if someone threatened to cut your throat if you didn't give up your belief you would say to them, "No! I would rather die rather than deny my belief in Allah." No, it's the only option we have, whatever our situation, alive or dead. Because it's only by belief that we can enter the Garden, and only by it that we can have ease in the grave, and only by it we can reach the highest ranks of the Garden. If we lose our belief we lose everything. All good comes from belief.

Who believes in Allah and His words

It was necessary, even for him 🕌 to have belief. There were certain things that Allah hid from Sayyidina Muhammad but he believed in them. For instance the Essence of the Real *ta'ala*, which is known only to Allah. And neither we nor the Prophets and Messengers know anything about the subtle intricacies of Allah's governance of His creation. All that can be said is that the inability to perceive it is perception. Nothing and no one is capable of grasping it. They only grasp a little according to the level of their intellect and what Allah opens up to them. And Sayyidina Muhammad ﷺ is the most knowledgeable of all those who have knowledge of Allah. There's no one else who gets anywhere near him, no other Prophet or Messenger or angel; yet in spite of that he says ﷺ: *"My Lord, increase me in knowledge."* (20:114) when he was all the time ascending endlessly through all the realms of knowledge.

And follow him so that hopefully you will be guided

"Follow him!" Let's stop there. *"And follow him so that hopefully you will be guided."* That's in belief, which we have; and we know that through good actions we can rise up through the levels of the Garden. So what do we need? Belief and following. If we believe but we don't follow it with action we expose ourselves to destruction. Allah has ordered us to take great care of our prayers, Allah has ordered us, if we have any wealth, to pay *zakat* on it and Allah has ordered us, if we are able to do it, to go on hajj. Allah has ordered us to do all these things so it's obligatory on us to carry them out. And if we don't do that we will find we've gone badly wrong. Anyhow Allah says: *"And follow him so that hopefully you will be guided."* *"Hopefully"* in this context means that we will definitely be guided, because everyone who follows Sayyidina Muhammad ﷺ, they are truly guided. They won't do anything except what will bring them closer to Allah.

I ask Allah to give us and you success in doing what He loves and is pleasing to Him. Let's leave it here today. I'm a little unwell; I'm just doing what I can with you. But I ask Allah to give me strength so I can carry on doing that a little bit longer.

3

al-A'raf 160 – 162

وَقَطَّعْنَٰهُمُ ٱثْنَتَىْ عَشْرَةَ أَسْبَاطًا أُمَمًا وَأَوْحَيْنَآ إِلَىٰ مُوسَىٰٓ إِذِ
ٱسْتَسْقَىٰهُ قَوْمُهُۥٓ أَنِ ٱضْرِب بِّعَصَاكَ ٱلْحَجَرَ فَٱنۢبَجَسَتْ مِنْهُ ٱثْنَتَا
عَشْرَةَ عَيْنًا قَدْ عَلِمَ كُلُّ أُنَاسٍ مَّشْرَبَهُمْ وَظَلَّلْنَا عَلَيْهِمُ ٱلْغَمَٰمَ
وَأَنزَلْنَا عَلَيْهِمُ ٱلْمَنَّ وَٱلسَّلْوَىٰ كُلُوا۟ مِن طَيِّبَٰتِ مَا
رَزَقْنَٰكُمْ وَمَا ظَلَمُونَا وَلَٰكِن كَانُوٓا۟ أَنفُسَهُمْ يَظْلِمُونَ ۝
وَإِذْ قِيلَ لَهُمُ ٱسْكُنُوا۟ هَٰذِهِ ٱلْقَرْيَةَ وَكُلُوا۟ مِنْهَا حَيْثُ شِئْتُمْ
وَقُولُوا۟ حِطَّةٌ وَٱدْخُلُوا۟ ٱلْبَابَ سُجَّدًا نَّغْفِرْ لَكُمْ
خَطِيٓـَٰٔتِكُمْ سَنَزِيدُ ٱلْمُحْسِنِينَ ۝ فَبَدَّلَ ٱلَّذِينَ ظَلَمُوا۟ مِنْهُمْ
قَوْلًا غَيْرَ ٱلَّذِى قِيلَ لَهُمْ فَأَرْسَلْنَا عَلَيْهِمْ رِجْزًا مِّنَ ٱلسَّمَآءِ
بِمَا كَانُوا۟ يَظْلِمُونَ ۝

*We divided them up into twelve tribes – communities. We
revealed to Musa when his people asked him for water: "Strike
the rock with your staff." Twelve fountains flowed out from it
and all the people knew their drinking place. And We shaded
them with clouds and sent down manna and quails to them:
"Eat of the good things We have provided you with." They did
not wrong Us; rather it was themselves they wronged. When they
were told: "Live in this town and eat of it wherever you like and*

say, 'Relieve us of our burdens!' and enter the gate prostrating. Your mistakes will be forgiven you. We will grant increase to the good-doers." But those of them who did wrong substituted words other than those they had been given. So We sent a plague on them from heaven for their wrongdoing. (7:160-162)

Allah *ta'ala* says in His Noble book: *"We divided them up into twelve tribes – communities."* Allah *ta'ala* is here talking about Bani Isra'il. He says that He divided them into twelve *asbat*, which is the plural of *sibt* and a *sibt* is a family grouping, a tribe. So Bani Isra'il were divided into twelve tribes and they were all under the authority of Sayyidina Musa.

We revealed to Musa when his people asked him for water: "Strike the rock with your staff." Twelve fountains flowed out from it and all the people knew their drinking place."

During a drought, Bani Isra'il came to Sayyidina Musa, to ask him to pray for rain for their crops. Allah ordered Musa to strike a rock with his staff. And from this rock twelve springs gushed out and Musa ordered a tribe to go to each of the springs so that each one had its own portion of the *baraka* of Sayyidina Musa and each had its own share of the water and each knew its own place for getting drinking water. So there was no fighting over the water because they each had a share. Then Allah ordered them to go to Quds (Jerusalem) but they refused and so He caused them to wander about in the desert for forty years. When the sun was burning them during these forty years of wandering Allah provided them with shade.

And We shaded them with clouds and sent down manna and quails to them:

A quail is a small bird and manna is something with a milk base which resembles cheese.

"Eat of the good things We have provided you with."

So they had meat in the form of quails and also the manna, and they ate only these for forty years. During this time of wandering Sayyidina Harun died. Because he died before Sayyidina Musa some of the Jews said that Sayyidina Musa killed him. This was because Sayyidina Musa was very strict and when he saw something wrong he would try to correct it. Sayyidina Harun was very easy going and for this reason was more acceptable to Bani Isra'il than Sayyidina Musa, so some of the Bani Isra'il claimed that Sayyidina Musa had killed Sayyidina Harun, saying, "You killed him because we loved him."

When Sayyidina Musa arrived at Jerusalem, he found some angels digging a grave about forty steps outside it and said to them, "I like this grave, it is pleasing to me." They said, "If you like it then come down and see if it fits you." And when he climbed down into it Allah *ta'ala* took his spirit there and then. So Sayyidina Musa is not buried in Jerusalem itself but a short distance outside of it. The grave of Sayyidina Musa can be found forty steps from the outer wall of Quds. Sayyidina Harun died and was buried during the forty years of wandering.

They did not wrong Us; rather it was themselves they wronged.

They disobeyed the commands of Allah and did the opposite of what He asked them to. When He said to them that they could recite the Torah from the scrolls or by heart and told them to pray in the synagogue or at home, they said, "We will only read the Torah from the scrolls and we will only pray in a synagogue." All of this was going against Allah *ta'ala*. Whatever Allah made easy for them they made difficult for themselves. In the *shari'a* of Sayyidina Muhammad you can pray in the mosque or at home, even though it is better to pray in the mosque. That is because our way is based on the mercy of Allah *ta'ala*. It is not rigid. As Allah *ta'ala* says regarding the Prophet ﷺ: "*We have only sent you as a mercy to all the worlds.*" (21:107) So by the *baraka* of Sayyidina Muhammad ﷺ Allah *ta'ala* made all the burden which the Bani Isra'il used to bear very light for us.

When they were told: "Live in this town and eat of it wherever you like and say, 'Relieve us of our burdens!' and enter the gate prostrating."

The town referred to here is Jerusalem. Allah *ta'ala* told them to enter the gate in humility and prostrate on entering it. In all of this Bani Isra'il went against the orders of Allah *ta'ala*. Therefore Allah *ta'ala* did not forgive them. They did not enter in state of prostration, they disobeyed Allah and this is why they are full of hatred for us, as Allah tells us: "*You will find that the people most hostile to the believers are the Jews and the idolaters.*" (5:82) The Christians are not so bad, as Allah says of them: "*You will find the people most affectionate to those who have iman are those who say, 'We are Christians.'*" (5:82) So Allah *ta'ala* has described how they, the Christians, react to the Muslims. And some Christians did become Muslims. Christians are near to the *deen* of Allah *ta'ala*, as they love the path of Allah. But they have to be brought to it by a teaching shaykh. If they had such a one they would know the truth of Allah *ta'ala* and reflect upon it and accept it.

"Your mistakes will be forgiven you. We will grant increase to the good-doers."

Therefore, there is no doubt that anyone who obeys Allah and keeps away from what Allah has forbidden is given increase. Allah *ta'ala* says in another *ayah*: *"If you are grateful I will certainly give you increase."* (14:7) It is obligatory to increase one's gratitude to Allah. And giving thanks to Allah *ta'ala* is not merely a matter of the tongue. Giving thanks to Allah is divided into three kinds: thankfulness of the tongue, thankfulness of the limbs and thankfulness of the heart. Thankfulness of the tongue is demonstrated by doing a lot of *dhikr* of Allah *ta'ala*. Thankfulness of the limbs is demonstrated by keeping them from wrong action and employing them in doing what Allah *ta'ala* has commanded and in the worship of Allah *ta'ala*. Thankfulness of the heart is demonstrated by witnessing and affirming all the bounties and blessings of Allah *ta'ala* and truly seeing them as coming directly from Him. As Allah *ta'ala* says in the Quran: *"Any blessing you have is from Allah."* (16:53) Since every blessing and good thing comes from Allah, do not say it is from me or it is from this or that. And know that when you are fasting and about to break your fast and you see Allah's blessings in front of you, and the great variety of Allah's blessings, know it is all from Allah *ta'ala*.

So gratitude to Allah takes three forms, that of the tongue, which is to do *dhikr* of Allah, that of the limbs which is to stop them from going towards wrong action and to push them towards right action, and that of the heart which is to recognise that every blessing you have is from Allah. And if Allah has given you something, take benefit from it. If He has given you the use of your tongue then use it well. We know, for instance, that if you bless the Prophet ﷺ once, then Allah blesses you ten times and if you bless the Prophet ﷺ ten times then Allah *ta'ala* blesses you a hundred times. We shouldn't be among the losers but should use our tongues in this way. Beware of these Wahhabis today who say, "No don't do *salat ala'n-nabi'* or anything like that." What I say is – do anything that will bring you near to Allah *ta'ala*, and leave everything that takes you away from Him. Allah says: *"We will grant increase to all good-doers."* If you do something good or if you are on the path of good then Allah *ta'ala* will certainly give you more.

But those of them who did wrong substituted words other than those they had been given. So We sent a plague on them from heaven for their wrongdoing.

This is a renewal of punishment from Allah *ta'ala* to Bani Isra'il because they kept on acting in a way contrary to what He had ordered them to do.

Ask them about the town which was by the sea

We'll look at this tomorrow, *insha'allah*. The Prophet ﷺ said to us that we should adopt four traits: two of which gain the pleasure of Allah and two of which we cannot do without. The two traits which please Allah are worshipping Him and not associating anything with him. So make sure that the aim of your actions is the Face of Allah, not doing things so that you will be given something in return, that puts you in danger: *"They were only*

ordered to worship Allah, making their deen sincerely His." 98:5
Your actions must be for the sake of Allah alone. This is what we
will be asked about and this will be the important thing for us on
the Day of Rising.

So we must worship Him and not associate anything with Him,
not commit *shirk*. And you know what *shirk* is, don't you? With us
shirk is of two sorts – and make sure you understand this – there
is hidden *shirk* and open *shirk*. Open *shirk* is when people worship
statues and idols, thinking that they will benefit them, that they
can harm them and give to them and prevent them from getting
things, like the idolaters of Makka. They had idols and thought
that they harmed them and benefitted them. That kind of *shirk*
is open and – no doubt about it – people who do that are in the
Fire forever. *"Allah does not forgive anything being associated with
Him."* 4:48

But there is also hidden *shirk* and that is to attribute effects
to their causes. Allah *ta'ala* has set up causes and effects but the
reality is that effects merely accompany the causes, they are not
brought about by them. In all the things that happen to us, Allah
is the doer. *"Allah created both you and what you do."* 37:96 He
created your actions. Where good things are concerned we ascribe
them to Allah; any bad things, we ascribe those to ourselves. So
in the case of all the things which are good and right we ascribe
them to our Lord. He is the One who helps us, provides for us,
gives to us, keeps evil away from us, all this we ascribe to Allah.
But in the case of bad actions we say that we are the ones who
disobeyed, we are the ones who did wrong, and we ask Allah to
accept our repentance from us and forgive us. It is necessary for
every human being to be clear about this.

We will finish there today. May Allah give us and you success in doing what is good and take us and you by the hand.

4

al-A'raf 163 – 167

وَسْـَٔلْهُمْ عَنِ ٱلْقَرْيَةِ ٱلَّتِى كَانَتْ حَاضِرَةَ ٱلْبَحْرِ إِذْ
يَعْدُونَ فِى ٱلسَّبْتِ إِذْ تَأْتِيهِمْ حِيتَانُهُمْ يَوْمَ سَبْتِهِمْ شُرَّعًا
وَيَوْمَ لَا يَسْبِتُونَ لَا تَأْتِيهِمْ كَذَٰلِكَ نَبْلُوهُم بِمَا كَانُوا۟
يَفْسُقُونَ ۝ وَإِذْ قَالَتْ أُمَّةٌ مِّنْهُمْ لِمَ تَعِظُونَ قَوْمًا ٱللَّهُ مُهْلِكُهُمْ أَوْ
مُعَذِّبُهُمْ عَذَابًا شَدِيدًا قَالُوا۟ مَعْذِرَةً إِلَىٰ رَبِّكُمْ وَلَعَلَّهُمْ يَتَّقُونَ ۝
فَلَمَّا نَسُوا۟ مَا ذُكِّرُوا۟ بِهِۦٓ أَنجَيْنَا ٱلَّذِينَ يَنْهَوْنَ عَنِ ٱلسُّوٓءِ وَأَخَذْنَا ٱلَّذِينَ
ظَلَمُوا۟ بِعَذَابٍۭ بِـَٔيسٍۭ بِمَا كَانُوا۟ يَفْسُقُونَ ۝ فَلَمَّا عَتَوْا۟ عَن مَّا نُهُوا۟ عَنْهُ
قُلْنَا لَهُمْ كُونُوا۟ قِرَدَةً خَٰسِـِٔينَ ۝ وَإِذْ تَأَذَّنَ رَبُّكَ لَيَبْعَثَنَّ عَلَيْهِمْ وَإِلَىٰ يَوْمِ
ٱلْقِيَٰمَةِ مَن يَسُومُهُمْ سُوٓءَ ٱلْعَذَابِ إِنَّ رَبَّكَ لَسَرِيعُ ٱلْعِقَابِ وَإِنَّهُۥ لَغَفُورٌ
رَّحِيمٌ ۝

Ask them about the town which was by the sea when they
broke the Sabbath – when their fish came to them near the
surface on their Sabbath day but did not come on the days
which were not their Sabbath. In this way We put them to the
test because they were deviators. When a group of them said,
'Why do you rebuke a people whom Allah is going to destroy or
severely punish?' they said, 'So that we have an excuse to present
to your Lord, and so that hopefully they will gain taqwa.' Then

when they forgot what they had been reminded of, We rescued those who had forbidden the evil and seized those who did wrong with a harsh punishment because they were deviators. When they were insolent about what they had been forbidden to do, We said to them, 'Be apes, despised, cast out!' Then your Lord announced that He would send against them until the Day of Rising people who would inflict an evil punishment on them. Your Lord is Swift in Retribution. And He is Ever-Forgiving, Most Merciful.

Allah *ta'ala* says in His Noble book: *"Ask them about the town which was by the sea…"* As we know this *ayah* is from *Surat al-A'raf* which was revealed to the Prophet 🌸 in *Makkah al-Mukarramah* except for this coming passage, which came down to the Prophet 🌸 in *Madina al-Munawwarah*. We know this because the Jews were only in Madina and this *ayah* is about the scheming of Bani Isra'il. These Jews were in fact descendants of those who were with Musa, *'alayhi's-salam*, but in this *ayah* Allah *ta'ala* addresses them as if they were their ancestors. The Prophet 🌸 started talking to these Jewish descendants about what their ancestors used to do. Although they were not doing exactly what their forefathers used to, one thing was sure: whatever was in their forefathers was also in them! They had inherited the negative qualities of their forbears. The Prophet 🌸 reminded them of their forefathers and what they were doing. This is why Allah *ta'ala* says:

and ask them concerning the town

Of course the question is not really about the town, it is really about the inhabitants of the town. And the inhabitants of that town were the ancestors of the Jews of Madina. According to the *mufassirun* the town was called Ayla or Madyan. It was by the sea and Allah *ta'ala* had forbidden the Jews to fish on Saturday, their Sabbath day. However, on Saturday the fish used to come close to the shore and the Jews saw this happening and, although Allah had forbidden them to fish on that day, they still wanted to get the fish. So they designed a way to catch the fish, thus disobeying Allah *ta'ala* and becoming *maghdubi alayhim* – among those upon whom Allah's anger alighted. They used to use ropes and put nets out and leave them there until Sunday, using this subterfuge to catch fish on the Sabbath.

Allah was showing the Prophet ﷺ what the Jews were; their behaviour, their innate disposition; how their behaviour was towards Allah *ta'ala* and how it was likely to be towards the Prophet ﷺ. Allah calls them *fasiqin* from the word *fisq* which means to go out from obedience to Allah *ta'ala* and they did this by devising this trick to catch fish on the Saturday and collect them on the Sunday. Allah says about what happened: *They broke the Sabbath – when their fish came to them near the surface on their Sabbath day but did not come on the days which were not their Sabbath. In this way We put them to the test because they were deviators – fasiqin.*

So this was a test for the *iman* of the Jews. They were forbidden to take the fish but, by devising this trick, they openly disobeyed Allah *ta'ala,* doing what He had ordered them not to do. So they showed that they were clearly disobedient. Allah wanted to test them to see whether they would be on the right path or not. If there is a lesson for the Jews in this then there is also a lesson for us in it as well. As certain things were allowed for them and certain things were forbidden, in the same way certain things are allowed for us and certain things are forbidden So we can only suppose that what happened to them will also happen to us. If we obey Allah we will get a reward and if we disobey Him we will get a punishment. Allah *ta'ala* tells us in this *ayah* that those who disobeyed Allah were punished in the *dunya* and will also be punished in the *akhira*. So we must protect ourselves from *ma'sia* – from disobedience to Allah *ta'ala* – and we should never forget the punishment of the grave and in the *akhirah*. But if we refrain from doing wrong actions, Allah *ta'ala* will reward us and place us among the *salihin*.

When a group of them said, "Why do you rebuke a people whom Allah is going to destroy or severely punish?" they said, "So that we have an excuse to present to your Lord, so that hopefully they will become people of *taqwa*."

These people were divided into three groups. One group took the fish, one group remained silent and the third group asked why the others had done what Allah *ta'ala* had forbidden. The group that had fallen into disobedience of Allah by fishing on the Sabbath were treated as Allah has described in Quran and the group who asked why they were fishing were rewarded for doing that. But the *Sahaba* disagreed about the ones who remained silent. Ibn Abbas said that they should be joined with those who did the fishing but some of the *Sahaba* said that these people did not do the action; they did not fish; they did not disobey Allah *ta'ala*. But anyway we have the three groups: those who fished, those who counselled them not to fish and those who remained silent. Allah *ta'ala* turned those who fished into pigs and monkeys.

And He gave those who counselled them not to fish a generous reward. As for those who remained silent – and whether they were punished or not – on this point we will remain silent. We don't know whether they were included with the people who did right or the people who did wrong.

In the past, things of this sort have often happened. Some people have disobeyed Allah and some have remained silent about it and others have counselled them not to disobey. The Prophet ﷺ said that if you see something wrong you must try to change it with your hand or your tongue or your heart. So it depends on the type of silence, because if we cannot change something with our hand we should change it with our tongue and if we cannot change it with our tongue we should change it in our heart. We should inwardly say, "O Allah this is a wrong action", so that we avoid actually participating in the wrong action by our silence. In this way we save ourselves from it. The point is to pull out of wrong action in one of these ways either by the hand or the tongue or at least in the heart so as to be safe from it. So whether these people were on the safe side or not is a point of valid disagreement.

As Allah says elsewhere: *"Be fearful of trials which will not afflict solely those among you who do wrong."* (6:25) So these troubles don't only come to wrongdoers. They may come to anyone. Allah *ta'ala* has given us the means to fight this trouble and wrongdoing with our tongues, limbs and hearts. Some of the people of Allah say that the action of the heart may in fact be even more powerful than the action of the hand or the tongue. It is very possible that when a person gets up in the night and turns to Allah and says to Allah, "O Allah this *fitna* has fallen upon us!" and he recognises Allah and asks for deliverance for the people and for himself, then by just doing that they are making a powerful action. This action may well be powerful enough to have real consequences within the course of their lifetime.

they said, "So that we have an excuse to present to your Lord, and so that hopefully they will gain *taqwa*."

This means that they turned to Allah *ta'ala* in order to free themselves from the actions which those other people were doing so as to be forgiven by Allah *ta'ala*. So their action was clear, to counsel the people of wrong action and obey the orders of Allah.

Then when they forgot what they had been reminded of, We rescued those who had forbidden the evil and seized those who did wrong with a harsh punishment because they were deviators.

So we come back to the three groups: those who acted wrongly, those who warned them and those who remained silent. Allah saved the second group, as this speaking out to prevent wrong has applied throughout all of the ages. Those who do it are always safe with Allah. And those who remained silent were also saved. As Allah says: *"We rescued those who had forbidden the evil..."* So as long as they rejected it in their hearts they were with those who had forbidden it with their tongues. But as for the wrongdoers, they were afflicted with a terrible punishment because they were *fasiqin* – people who deviated from the *deen*. The worst of them became pigs and the others monkeys. As Allah tells us: *"When they were insolent about what they had been forbidden to do, We said to them, 'Be apes, despised, cast out!'"* Those who were transformed in this way only remained alive for a short time after their transmogrification.

Then your Lord announced that He would send against them until the Day of Rising people who would inflict an evil punishment on them. Your Lord is Swift in Retribution. And He is Ever-Forgiving, Most Merciful.

As their intentions were treacherous and they wanted good for no one but themselves these people became exposed to punishment and persecution in this world throughout the ages. Allah is swift in wreaking retribution on His enemies and on the unbelievers and He is also Ever-forgiving and Most Merciful to His friends and to the believers.

I was saying a few things about Ramadan. One thing is that we have the time of the breaking of the fast. Every fasting person has a *du'a* guaranteed to be answered when he breaks his fast. So don't just say "*assalamu alaykum*" after maghrib, and start eating. There is a proper *adab* to breaking the fast. You should say: *"Allahumma laka sumtu wa bika amantu wa 'ala rizqika aftartu fa-ghfir li ma qaddamtu wa ma akhkhartu wa ma asrartu wa ma a'lantu"* – "O Allah, I have fasted for You and believed in You and broken my fast on provision from You so forgive me for anything I have done or left undone either in secret or openly" – and then pray Maghrib. Then after that, when you have eaten, you should make a *du'a* to Allah saying: *"Allahumma inni as'aluka ridaka wa'l-janna wa ma yuqarribu ilayhima min qawlin wa 'amal wa a'udhu bika min sakhatika wa-n-nar wa ma yuqarribu ilayhima min qawlin wa 'amal"* – "O Allah I ask You for Your good pleasure and the Garden and for words and actions that will bring them close to me and I seek refuge with You from Your anger and the Fire and words and actions that will bring them close to me". This is a very good *du'a* to make because it is asking for the best possible things, and remember you have one *du'a* which is guaranteed to be answered.

And you shouldn't overeat because the whole point of fasting is to cut down on eating too much. But if when people break their fast, they stuff themselves, it is as if they haven't fasted at all. Because the purpose of fasting is to discipline the *nafs*. You should eat a bit and then have some rest and at *sahur* it is vital to have something more to eat. There is the hadith: "Have *sahur* because there is a *baraka* in *sahur*. Allah and His angels pray for blessing on the people who have *sahur*." So you should definitely have something for *sahur*, even if it is just something light. Not just sleep through and not get up or you will lose out on an important *sunna*.

And you will also miss out on another time when your *du'a* is guaranteed to be answered, because at that time Allah asks about those who are asking Him for things so that He can respond to them, or seeking forgiveness from Him so that He can forgive them. That last third of the night, the *sahar* time, is full to the brim with good. It is not a time anyone should sleep through. Allah *ta'ala* descends during it and says, "Is there any asker there so that I can give to him, or anyone seeking forgiveness so that I can forgive him, anyone repenting so that I can turn towards him, anyone wanting My pardon…" until dawn comes and then the door of Allah's treasury shuts. No one must waste that time. So have something to eat for *sahur* and turn to your Lord during that time.

5

al-A'raf 7:168-171

وَقَطَّعْنَٰهُمْ فِى ٱلْأَرْضِ أُمَمًا مِّنْهُمُ ٱلصَّٰلِحُونَ وَمِنْهُمْ دُونَ ذَٰلِكَ وَبَلَوْنَٰهُم بِٱلْحَسَنَٰتِ وَٱلسَّيِّـَٔاتِ لَعَلَّهُمْ يَرْجِعُونَ ۝ فَخَلَفَ مِنۢ بَعْدِهِمْ خَلْفٌ وَرِثُوا۟ ٱلْكِتَٰبَ يَأْخُذُونَ عَرَضَ هَٰذَا ٱلْأَدْنَىٰ وَيَقُولُونَ سَيُغْفَرُ لَنَا وَإِن يَأْتِهِمْ عَرَضٌ مِّثْلُهُۥ يَأْخُذُوهُ أَلَمْ يُؤْخَذْ عَلَيْهِم مِّيثَٰقُ ٱلْكِتَٰبِ أَن لَّا يَقُولُوا۟ عَلَى ٱللَّهِ إِلَّا ٱلْحَقَّ وَدَرَسُوا۟ مَا فِيهِ وَٱلدَّارُ ٱلْءَاخِرَةُ خَيْرٌ لِّلَّذِينَ يَتَّقُونَ أَفَلَا تَعْقِلُونَ ۝ وَٱلَّذِينَ يُمَسِّكُونَ بِٱلْكِتَٰبِ وَأَقَامُوا۟ ٱلصَّلَوٰةَ إِنَّا لَا نُضِيعُ أَجْرَ ٱلْمُصْلِحِينَ ۝ وَإِذْ نَتَقْنَا ٱلْجَبَلَ فَوْقَهُمْ كَأَنَّهُۥ ظُلَّةٌ وَظَنُّوٓا۟ أَنَّهُۥ وَاقِعٌۢ بِهِمْ خُذُوا۟ مَآ ءَاتَيْنَٰكُم بِقُوَّةٍ وَٱذْكُرُوا۟ مَا فِيهِ لَعَلَّكُمْ تَتَّقُونَ ۝

And We divided them into communities in the earth. Some of them are right-acting and some are other than that. We tried them with good and evil so that hopefully they would return. An evil generation has succeeded them, inheriting the Book, taking the goods of this lower world, and saying, "We will be forgiven." But if similar goods come to them again they still take them. Has not a covenant been made with them in the Book, that they should only say the truth about Allah and have they not studied what is in it? The Final Abode is better for those who have taqwa. Will you not use your intellect? As for those who hold fast to the Book and establish the prayer, We will not let the wage of right-acting people be wasted. When We uprooted the mountain, lifting it above them like a canopy, and they thought it was about to fall on them: "Seize hold vigorously of what We have given you and remember what is in it, so that hopefully you will have taqwa." (7:168:171)

Allah *ta'ala* says in His Mighty Book: *"And We divided them into communities on the earth."* We have already told you that this *surah* is called *Suratu'l-A'raf* and was revealed to the Prophet ﷺ in the noble city of Makka, except for these *ayahs* which we are looking at which came down to the Prophet ﷺ in Madina. We know this because there were no Jews in Makka, only idolaters, whereas there were Jews in Madina, and all round it – for instance in Khaybar and places like that. These places were all inhabited by Jews. So all the references in the Qur'an concerning the Jews were revealed in Madina.

And We divided them into communities on the earth.

This is an example of Allah telling us about unseen things in the future because the Jews have never again been able to unify themselves as a nation. Allah says: *"We divided them into communities,"* meaning that Allah, *tabaraka wa ta'ala*, put some of them in every country; in each country you find a group. They will never be truly unified again. They have started to gather in Palestine but before that some were in France, some in Britain, some in America and various other countries. They were all over the place in groups but not together. Even though they are now gathering in Palestine, they will never again become a geographically unified nation. Allah says: *"We divided them into communities in the earth,"* referring to those who did not follow Sayyidina Musa, *'alayhi salam* properly. No! rather they disobeyed what they were ordered to do in the Torah.

Some of them are right-acting.

This refers to the ones who followed Sayyidina Musa 🕮 respecting what he brought and it also applies to those who died during the gap between Sayyidina Musa and Sayyidina Isa. Those who died during this gap are also called "right-acting". When there is a gap between Prophets and someone dies during that period as a person who affirms Allah's unity they will not enter the Fire. This is because there was no Prophet there to be rejected. However, what about those who were alive during the life-time of Sayyidina Isa 🕮 and did not follow him, what category do they fall under? They are unbelievers because Allah sent Sayyidina Isa after Sayyidina Musa 🕮. Then after that Allah sent Sayyidina Muhammad 🕮 and only a very small number of Jews followed Sayyidina Muhammad 🕮 – among them were 'Abdallah ibn Salam and Ka'b al-Ahbar. These are two Jews who followed Sayyidina Muhammad 🕮.

When Abdallah ibn Salam became Muslim the other Jews did not know about his Islam. He went to the Messenger 🕮 and said, "I am a leader of my community and one of their scholars. I would like you to hide me and then bring them and ask them what they think of Abdallah ibn Salam. Then when they tell you and mention the respect they have for me, I will come out and say, 'I bear witness that there is no god but Allah and Muhammad is the Messenger of Allah.'" So the Messenger of Allah ﷺ did that. He summoned the heads of the Jews from Madina, Khaybar and the surrounding areas and he hid Abdallah ibn Salam from them. He asked them, "What do you say about this man Abdallah ibn Salam?" They said, "He is our master and the son of our master." He then asked them, "What would you say if he were to become a Muslim?" They said, "God forbid that he should ever become a Muslim." When they said that he came out and said the *shahada* and they immediately said, "He is our enemy and the son of our enemy." One minute they were saying he was their master and the son of their master and the next that he their enemy and the son of their enemy!

We divided them into communities in the earth.

Allah split them up among different countries and they will never really be unified. "*Some of them are right-acting*" – those who believed – "*and some are other than that*" – the unbelievers among them.

We tested them with good and evil...

What is meant by "good" here are all the good things Allah lavished on them, for example, plenty of rain, plenty of vegetation, and their trading and wealth. These things are the "good" they had. As for the "evil" that refers to the droughts and illnesses and other such hardships they suffered. These things are the "evil" referred to.

So that hopefully they would return.

So Allah tested them by lavishing good things on them, so they might return and hold to the Torah and the *deen* of Sayyidina

(Interruption "Muhammad") No, Sayyidina Musa, not Sayyidina Muhammad. We are talking about Sayyidina Musa at the moment. They disagreed regarding him as well. Then when Allah sent Sayyidina Muhammad ﷺ they all rejected him outright, with very few exceptions. Like Abdallah ibn Salam and Ka'b al-Ahbar and a few other Jews who followed the Prophet ﷺ.

A generation – *khalf* – has succeeded them, inheriting the book.

Here Allah *ta'ala* is describing what happened to them by using the word *khalf*. We have two words for a following generation: *khalf* and *khalaf* and they are opposite in meaning. The word *khalf* refers to descendants of bad character, an evil generation. They are called *khalf*. Then we also have the word *khalaf* which means descendants of good character, a good generation. For example, a man appoints a *khalaf* to succeed him. He is his *khalifa*, a good successor. But if they are other than that we call them *khalf*. They are successors of bad character. That is why Allah *ta'ala* uses the word *khalf* here.

Inheriting the Book.

What's the book referred to here? It's the Torah.

Taking the goods of this lower world.

People would come to them for judgment and then they would take bribes and change the laws which were in the Torah. Why did they do that? Out of pure greed.

and saying we will be forgiven.

And in one reading adding: "because we do not associate anything with Allah," because Allah does not forgive anything being associated with Him. Allah says: *"Allah does not forgive anything being associated with Him, but He forgives whoever He wills for anything other than that."* 4:47 But that only applies if they are really believers, not if they are idolaters or unbelievers, in that case there is no forgiveness. The only fate for an unbeliever is eternity in the Fire.

But if similar goods come to them again, they still take them. Has not a covenant been made with them in the Book, that they should only say the truth about Allah.

The truth referred to here is what Allah revealed in the Torah. Because their Book was the Torah, which Sayyidina Musa received from Allah, *ta'ala*. This Torah is a tremendous thing. Allah says: *"We sent down the Torah, containing guidance and light, and the Prophets who had submitted themselves gave judgment by it for the Jews – as did their scholars and their rabbis – by what they had been allowed to preserve of Allah's Book to which they were witnesses."* 5:44 In any case the Torah contains great knowledges and secrets but it became corrupted! Things were added to it and deleted from it and altered in it according to what suited the whims and desires of the people at that time and they abandoned things which didn't suit them.

and have they not studied what is in it? The Final Abode is better for those who have *taqwa*.

This advice applies to both them and us. This is something that also applies to us Muslims. Allah *ta'ala* says here: *"The Final Abode is better for those who have taqwa."* Those people who have *taqwa* and have fear of Allah, they don't go along with bribery, for instance, because Allah has ordained that the practitioners of bribery, if they don't repent, that they too will have an immense punishment. Because bribery means that the rich have an unfair advantage and can escape justice and if someone is poor he cannot get justice and will suffer injustice. That's what bribery does.

The Final abode is better for those who have *taqwa*.

You know what *taqwa* is don't you? We have said on many occasions that *taqwa* consists in following Allah's commands and avoiding His prohibitions. *"Whatever the Messenger gives you you should accept and whatever he forbids you you should forgo."* 59:7 Allah has ordered us to pray and pay *zakat* and fast and go on Hajj, and to protect our limbs from wrong actions and, most important of all, to protect our hearts from envy and rancour and pride. If a person is free of this he possesses every good thing, every good thing.

Will you not use your intellect?

This is a warning from Allah telling us that the purpose of the intellect is to understand what will bring us nearer to Allah and so act on it, and to understand what will distance us from Allah and so avoid it. Anyone with intellect uses it to understand things. If someone has real intellect they will use it to understand what brings them close to Allah and they will act on that. And as for the things that they know will distance them from Allah, they know that repayment in the Next World is certainly coming. All of us are going to die. Allah tells us: *"Every self will taste death."* 3:185 and *"Everyone on it will pass away; but the Face of your Lord will remain, Master of Majesty and Generosity."* 55:24-25 and *"All things are passing except His Face."* 28:88

If a person is really aware of their approaching death and what comes after death, such as the Reckoning and the *Sirat* and the Balance, and knows that they themselves will have to go through this, it will certainly have a real effect on them. If someone takes these things to heart they will know that when they die there is punishment in the grave and that they will be examined at the Resurrection, and on the *Sirat* and at the Balance. These are big tests. But if Allah takes you by the hand, you will reflect and say, "Death is definitely something which will come to me. That is clear! And after it comes the Resurrection and after that the *Sirat*, and the Balance. And after all those things there is either the Garden or the Fire." If someone knows this, and confirms it and believes it, they will certainly prepare for it. But if they waste their time ignoring this reality, not realising what's really going on, not being aware of their death and what comes after it, they're going to be in real trouble when they die. They will have trouble in their grave and at their rising from the grave and on the *Sirat*. All of us are going to have to face these things. That's why Allah says: *"Will you not use your intellect?"* The purpose of the intellect to reflect on what will benefit us and bring us closer to Allah.

As for those who hold fast to the Book

Those who hold fast to the Book in this context are the people who truly grasped the Torah and acted on it. This *ayah*, however, also refers to us, because everything that is revealed concerning past peoples also applies to us. The commands and prohibitions they were subject to also apply to us, even if there are some differences. Those who hold fast to the Book are those who obey its commands and avoid its prohibitions.

and establish the prayer

Allah doesn't say just "do the prayer"; He makes a distinction between doing the prayer and establishing it. Not everyone who does the prayer establishes it. Establishment includes, for instance, freeing oneself from impurities. This underlies the act of prayer. Everything is built on freeing oneself from impurity. For instance someone might have urine on him when he does *wudu*. But the whole purification process is based on being free from urine and so his *wudu* is useless. And once that basic purification is in place then you have to be absolutely correct in your *wudu*. You mustn't leave any dry spot on either your face, or your arms or your feet. That's why Allah *ta'ala* says: "*establish the prayer.*"

And after you have finished *wudu* you must give the prayer its full due. Do the *takbir al-ihram* with majesty, and the recitation with clarity, and do *ruku* until you achieve stillness, and say three times, "*subhana'llahi wa bihamdihi, subhana'llahi'l-'adhim*" and if you want to to give full measure say, "*subhana'llahi wa bihamdihi 'adada khalqihi wa rida nafsihi wa zinata 'arshihi wa midada kalamatih*" that's even better. It encompasses a huge benefit. And likewise in *sujud*, "*subhana rabbi'l'ala wa bi hamdihi 'adada khalqihi wa rida nafsihi wa zinata 'arshihi wa midada kalamatih*". Allah gives a tremendous reward for this *tasbih*.

We will not let the wage of the *salihun* go to waste.

If someone is *salih*, putting both himself and other people right, Allah will not fail to reward them. It is incumbent on every human being to put himself right, and his children and his wife and his close relations, "All of you are shepherds and all of you are responsible for your flock." Don't only think about yourself. If your family don't pray – and maybe don't even fast – tomorrow on the Day of Rising you will be questioned about that, and also about your children who are living with you: "All of you are shepherds and all of you are responsible for your flock." When they come back from school should ask them if they have prayed and if not remind them that they should pray. If you're not firm with them they will never have any *deen*; if you don't remind them they won't do anything.

When We uprooted the mountain, lifting it above them like a canopy,

No, not that yet; we still haven't finished with the previous *ayah*. When people die, if their actions are good, they take on a beautiful form and have a beautiful aroma. They will ask, "Who are you?" The beautiful form will reply, "I am your right actions, and I am going to keep you company until you enter the Garden." And if, and we seek refuge with Allah from it, someone's actions are bad, they take on a hideous form and have a foul stench. A terrifying appearance. They will say, "Get away from me." The monstrous form will reply, "What do you mean get away from you? I am your actions. You are the one who made me look like this." Everyone's actions enter their grave with them, if they are right actions they will be a comfort to them, if they are other than that they will torment them. So everyone should be aware of that.

Before you go to sleep you should always say: *"astaghfirullah al-'adhim alladhi la ilaha illahu al-hayyu'l-qayyumu wa atubu ilayhi,"*

105

three times. There is a *sahih hadith* which says: "Whoever goes to bed and says *'astaghfirullah al-'adhim ladhi la ilaha illahu al-hayyu'l-qayyumu wa atubu ilayhi,'* three times, his wrong actions will be forgiven even if they are as much as the froth on the sea, the grains of sand on the shore, the days of this world and all the leaves on all the trees." This *istighfar* should be said by people, how many times? Before sleeping, three times. There is no need to do it any more than that. This a hadith and it is *sahih*, recorded by the two shaykhs: "Whoever goes to bed and says *'astaghfirullah al-'adhim ladhi la ilaha illahu al-hayyu'l-qayyumu wa atubu ilayhi,'* three times, his wrong actions will be forgiven even if they are as much as the froth on the sea, the grains of sand on the shore, the days of this world and all the leaves on all the trees."

When We uprooted the mountain, lifting it above them like a canopy.

This is one of the things Allah did to discipline Bani Isra'il. When He ordered them to follow the Torah and they disobeyed Him, Allah ordered that mountain to hover above them, He lifted it over their heads. If Allah had ordered it to fall on them, it would have done so and crushed them. He lifted it over them like a canopy and it stayed up there. It was waiting for the order, whether to fall on them and crush them, or not. But Allah just did it to frighten them and didn't send the mountain crashing down on top of them. But they were frightened and some of them returned to the *deen* and held fast to the Torah, and some of them, and we ask Allah's protection from that, stayed as they were.

and they thought that it was about to fall on them.

It was on the point of falling on them but then Allah was kind to them and just caused them fear through it. Some of them returned to the truth and believed in Sayyidina Musa and acted on the Torah; and some of them remained hypocrites.

Seize hold vigorously of what We have given you,

Now this command, in the same way that it applied to Bani Isra'il, also applies to us. It is incumbent on us as well to seize hold vigorously of the Book, in our case the Qur'an, in other words not neglect any of it. Wherever there is a command we have to comply with it and wherever them there is a prohibition we have to observe it. This doesn't just apply to Bani Isra'il. Any *surah* or command directed at any previous peoples also applies to us.

Seize hold vigorously of what We have given you,

Vigorously not feebly! Don't do the prayer "da, da, da, da, *assalamu 'alaykum*" and that's it! Give it its full due. And safeguard the fast properly, standing in the night in prayer and doing all those things which bring you nearer to Allah. Do these things with energy and vigour, in the knowledge that you are just a traveller passing through this world. Here we all are, sitting here today, but where have all the previous generations gone? All gone back to Allah. In any case it is clear that in death we have a powerful reminder. Allah commands us to remember death and what comes after death; but if we stay wrapped up in this world and our appetites and think of nothing else but that, and are only concerned with working for this world, when we get to the Next World we will find ourselves utterly bankrupt. Allah *ta'ala* says: *"Whatever good you send ahead for yourselves you will find it with Allah as something better and as a greater reward."* 2:109 *"Those who produce a good action will receive ten like it,"* 6:161 or indeed up to seventy like it: *"Allah gives such multiplied increase to whoever He wills."* 2:160

and remember what is in it, so that hopefully you will have taqwa.

We talked about *taqwa* earlier. Allah mentions *taqwa* in His Book in relation to certain things. So anyone who wants knowledge has to have *taqwa* as well. Allah says: *"Have taqwa of Allah and Allah will give you knowledge."* 2:281 Those students who pray and have fear of Allah, Allah will open the doors of knowledge for them straight away. Because Allah says: *"Have taqwa of Allah and Allah will give you knowledge."* 2:281 But the door of knowledge will never open for someone who doesn't pray or do *dhikrullah*, and spends all their time with heedless people or playing silly games or wasting their time like that.

and remember what is in it, so that hopefully you will have taqwa.

Allah *ta'ala* orders Bani Isra'il to remember what is in the Torah and to act by it and He orders us to reflect on the Qur'an and act by that. The meanings of the Qur'an embrace every other revelation. It includes what is in the Torah and what is in the Injil (Gospel) and what is in the Zabur (Psalms). All the Revealed Books have been gathered by Allah in the Qur'an. Just as Allah gathered together all good qualities in Sayyidina Muhammad ﷺ, he gathered together all good for us in the Book of Allah.

and remember what is in it, so that hopefully you will have taqwa.

We said that *taqwa* is obedience to all the commands of Allah and avoidance of all His prohibitions. The first stage of *taqwa* is knowledge of Allah. If you ask someone if they know Allah they say *la ilaha illa'llah*, but this *la ilaha illa'llah* has a meaning, and if someone says it they should know what it means, in order to really enter the land of *tawhid*. They must know Allah *tabaraka wa ta'ala* in the correct way, acknowledging the evidence for His existence, both empirical and intellectual. Allah *tabaraka wa ta'ala* commands us to affirm His Oneness and to gain knowledge of Him. This knowledge of him is of two kinds, one is based on evidence and proofs and the other comes from natural phenomena.

We might say to someone how did you get to know your Lord. They might reply, "I found my parents saying *la ilaha illa'llah* and so I said it." That is not enough. If someone says they know Allah they must produce something in support of that assertion. A person might, for instance, say that they did not exist and then their Lord nurtured them in their mother's womb and continued doing that until they emerged out into this world. Then He gave them milk to drink until they grew bigger. What is this called? This is empirical evidence for Allah's existence and it is sufficient. An Arab was asked how he knew his Lord and he was someone who knew about camels. So he replied that the dung *(ba'r)* indicates the camel *(ba'ir)* and footprints indicate a traveller. And as the poet said: "The sky with its constellations, and the earth with its plant-life, and the oceans with their waves, do they not indicate the All-penetrating, the All-aware." All of that indicates Allah.

Who raised up the sky? Who filled the oceans with water? Who makes the winds blow? Who makes the rain fall? Who makes the plants grow? These are all empirical evidence for the existence of Allah. Allah *ta'ala* revealed seven hundred *ayahs* in the Qur'an containing this type of evidence. *"Mankind worship your Lord, who created you and those before you, so that hopefully you will have taqwa. It is He Who made the earth a couch for you, and the sky a dome. He sends down water from the sky and by it brings forth fruits for your provision. Do not, then, knowingly make others equal to Allah."* 2:20-21 And: *"In the creation of the heavens and earth, and the alternation of the night and day, and the ships which sail the seas to people's benefit, and the water which Allah sends down from the sky — by which He brings the earth to life when it was dead and scatters about in it creatures of every kind — and the varying direction of the winds, and the clouds subservient between heaven and earth, there are Signs for people who use their intellect."* 2:163 And: *"Among His Signs is the creation of the heavens and earth and the variety of your languages and colours."* 30:21 All of us originate from a drop of sperm. So why is this one black and that one white, this one tall and that one short, this one clever and that one not? They are all manifestations of who? Of our Lord. And in that way they are all evidence of Allah, *subhanahu wa ta'ala*.

There are many many *ayahs* in the Qur'an outlining this empirical evidence for the Divine existence. But as for the intellectual evidence it is the logicians who talk about that. They bring, for example, the analogy of exception and the analogy of concurrence, and use linguistic analysis of Arabic. But this is beyond the scope of most of people. It is enough, in fact, just to have knowledge of yourself. You need only say to yourself, "Who gave me eyesight, enabling me to see? Who gave me hearing, enabling me to hear. Who gave me an intellect, enabling me to think." That is enough. It is what? It is empirical evidence for the Divine existence. This has all come from His words, *subhanahu wa ta'ala*: "*and remember what is in it, so that hopefully you will have taqwa.*"

Let's leave it there for the time being. I was saying a few words about Ramadan. We said to you that Ramadan is the storehouse of all the actions of the year. Why did we say that? It is because in it the *nafila* has the same status that the *fard* does at other times. So anyone who has missed a *fard* and does a lot of *nafilas* in Ramadan, then each *nafila* replaces a *fard*. If anyone does a voluntary action in Ramadan it counts as doing a *fard* at any other time and if anyone does a *fard* action it counts as seventy *fards* outside Ramadan. So we have a store of wealth in Ramadan which does not exist outside Ramadan. All of our actions are multiplied.

For this reason people should be especially on their guard. They should have all their faculties under control. The most important is the tongue because backbiting actually breaks the fast. The Companions said, "Messenger of Allah, what if what we say about someone is true?" He replied, "If you say that about him, that is backbiting." If you talk behind someone's back and say, for example, that he is a thief, and he actually is – it's not that he isn't, he really has got that bad quality – that is still backbiting. What you should do is advise him to his face: "My brother, I have great regard for you but I see things in you which other people might find objectionable. If Allah guides you and you turn to Your Lord and have recourse to Him, know that the door of *tawba* is always open." That's a good thing to do. But on the other hand, if you talk behind his back and say that so and so is a fool and doesn't know anything or keeps indulging in bad actions, and all of it is true, what is that called? It is backbiting. Allah ta'ala says: *"…and do not backbite one another. Would any of you like to eat his brother's dead flesh? No, you would hate it."* 49:12

We said that if someone does a *nafila* – and the night is long – if you do a *nafila* in Ramadan, it is the same as doing a *fard* in any other month. We have all got some shortcomings in respect of our *fards*; no one completely fulfils all the *fards* he has to do. How many people don't start praying till they are eighteen, how many till they are twenty? And some don't start till they are thirty. So all of us have something to make up. And if you want to do that then every *nafila* in Ramadan has the status of a *fard*.

We will finish there today. May Allah give us and you success in doing what is good and take us and you by the hand.

6

al-A'raf 7:171-178

خُذُوا مَآ ءَاتَيْنَـٰكُم بِقُوَّةٍ وَاذْكُرُوا مَا فِيهِ لَعَلَّكُمْ تَتَّقُونَ ۝ وَإِذْ أَخَذَ رَبُّكَ
مِنۢ بَنِىٓ ءَادَمَ مِن ظُهُورِهِمْ ذُرِّيَّتَهُمْ وَأَشْهَدَهُمْ عَلَىٰٓ أَنفُسِهِمْ أَلَسْتُ بِرَبِّكُمْ قَالُوا
بَلَىٰ شَهِدْنَآ أَن تَقُولُوا يَوْمَ الْقِيَـٰمَةِ إِنَّا كُنَّا عَنْ هَـٰذَا غَـٰفِلِينَ ۝ أَوْ تَقُولُوٓا
إِنَّمَآ أَشْرَكَ ءَابَآؤُنَا مِن قَبْلُ وَكُنَّا ذُرِّيَّةً مِّنۢ بَعْدِهِمْ ۖ أَفَتُهْلِكُنَا بِمَا فَعَلَ
الْمُبْطِلُونَ ۝ وَكَذَٰلِكَ نُفَصِّلُ الْـَٔايَـٰتِ وَلَعَلَّهُمْ يَرْجِعُونَ ۝ وَاتْلُ عَلَيْهِمْ
نَبَأَ الَّذِىٓ ءَاتَيْنَـٰهُ ءَايَـٰتِنَا فَانسَلَخَ مِنْهَا فَأَتْبَعَهُ الشَّيْطَـٰنُ فَكَانَ مِنَ
الْغَاوِينَ ۝ وَلَوْ شِئْنَا لَرَفَعْنَـٰهُ بِهَا وَلَـٰكِنَّهُۥٓ أَخْلَدَ إِلَى الْأَرْضِ وَاتَّبَعَ
هَوَىٰهُ ۚ فَمَثَلُهُۥ كَمَثَلِ الْكَلْبِ إِن تَحْمِلْ عَلَيْهِ يَلْهَثْ
أَوْ تَتْرُكْهُ يَلْهَث ۚ ذَّٰلِكَ مَثَلُ الْقَوْمِ الَّذِينَ كَذَّبُوا بِـَٔايَـٰتِنَا ۚ
فَاقْصُصِ الْقَصَصَ لَعَلَّهُمْ يَتَفَكَّرُونَ ۝ سَآءَ مَثَلًا الْقَوْمُ الَّذِينَ
كَذَّبُوا بِـَٔايَـٰتِنَا وَأَنفُسَهُمْ كَانُوا يَظْلِمُونَ ۝ مَن يَهْدِ اللَّهُ فَهُوَ
الْمُهْتَدِى ۖ وَمَن يُضْلِلْ فَأُو۟لَـٰٓئِكَ هُمُ الْخَـٰسِرُونَ ۝

"Seize hold vigorously of what We have given you and
remember what is in it, so that perhaps you will have taqwa."
When your Lord took out all their descendants from the
loins of the children of Adamand made them testify against
themselves: "Am I not your Lord?" They said, "We testify that

indeed You are!" Lest you say on the Day of Rising, "We were heedless of this." Or lest you say, "Our forefathers associated partners with Allah before our time, and we are merely descendants coming after them. So are You going to destroy us for what those purveyors of falsehood did?" That is how We mark out the Signs so that perhaps they will return. Recite to them the tale of him to whom We gave Our Signs, but who then cast them to one side and Shaytan caught up with him. He was one of those lured into error. If We had willed, We would have raised him up by them. But he gravitated towards the earth and pursued his whims and base desires. His likeness is that of a dog: if you chase it away, it lolls out its tongue and pants, and if you leave it alone, it lolls out its tongue and pants. That is the likeness of people who deny Our Signs. So tell the story so that perhaps they will reflect. How evil is the likeness of those who deny Our Signs. It is themselves whom they have badly wronged. Whoever Allah guides is truly guided. But those He misguides are the lost.

Allah *ta'ala* says in His Mighty Book: "*Seize hold vigorously of what We have given you and remember what is in it, so that hopefully you will have taqwa.*" This *ayah* was revealed about the Jews because they abandoned acting by the Torah. Consequently Allah ordered them to take hold of the Torah with seriousness and energy, but they were negligent about it and, as Allah tells us, a group of them disdainfully tossed the Book of Allah behind their backs, just as if they did not know, following their own whims and desires.

But this *ayah*, although it was revealed concerning the Jews, is also true for us. It is incumbent on us to take hold of the Qu'ran with seriousness and energy and to implement the commands in it and avoid its prohibitions and to take to heart what it tells us regarding the matters of the Next World – the Garden and the Fire and the *Sirat* and the Balance and the Basin and other such things. We shouldn't recite the Qur'an and then just go on as if we hadn't heard anything at all.

Seize hold vigorously of what We have given you and remember what is in it,

In other words pay attention to its admonitions, obey its commands and avoid its prohibitions. And what will the result of that be for us: *so that hopefully you will have taqwa.* This is because *taqwa* is obedience to the commands of Allah and avoidance of all His prohibitions. And Allah has made *taqwa* the cause of many benefits for us. Allah *ta'la* tells us: *"Whoever has taqwa of Allah – He will give him a way out and provide for him from where he does not expect."* 65:2-3 He also says: *"Have taqwa of Allah and Allah will give you knowledge."* 2:281 and: *"The people who have taqwa will be amid Gardens and Rivers, on seats of honour in the presence of an All-Powerful King."*

Taqwa is that your eyes should not look at *haram* things; your ears should not listen to backbiting and slander; your hands should not take anything which does not belong to you; and your feet should not walk to any inappropriate place, only to a place where there is benefit for you; but any place devoted to the wrong actions of usury, or slander, or wine or other such things, it is *haram* for you to go there. If you do, you will have the anger of Allah on you both going there and coming back. *Taqwa* gives us every good thing, in the sensory and the meaning. Whoever wants the profit of this world must have *taqwa*, and whoever wants the profit of the Next World must have *taqwa*. Then Allah goes on to mention certain matters relating to the world of the spirits. He says:

When your Lord took out all their descendants from the loins of the children of Adam…

Now these spirits we all have were in another world before we came into this one; they were in the world of the Unseen and they were totally conscious. And Allah spoke to them there. He ordered them to be believing and to affirm His unity, and to be right-acting *"and"* – as He continues –

made them testify against themselves…

What were they testifying about? They testified that they would affirm Allah's unity and be right-acting, obeying His commands and prohibitions.

"Am I not your Lord?"

He asked them this question: "Am I not your Lord?" He is affirming to us that He is indeed our Lord. And what is the meaning of "Lord". The word "Lord" has several meanings. It means "Putter right" or "Repairer" and it means the "One who nurtures everything through every stage of its existence". He takes us from being a drop of liquid in a man's loins which fertilizes an egg and is transferred to a woman's womb. He says, "Be a drop, then be a clot then be a lump and then be bones then, as Allah says He: *'clothes the bones in flesh; and then brings him into being as another creature. Blessed be Allah, the Best of Creators! Then subsequently you will certainly die. Then on the Day of Rising you will be raised again.'"* 23:14-16 That whole process is all contained within the meaning of the Arabic word *rabb* or "Lord".

Allah mentions the word *rabb* in many *ayahs*. He begins His Book with the words: *"al-hamdu lillahi rabbi 'l-'alamin."* It is as if the word *rabb* gathers together all His attributes. Because you cannot have a *rabb* who is not powerful, willing, knowing, living, hearing, seeing and speaking, gathering together all the attributes of perfection and being free of any defects which are not appropriate to Lordship. The Lord is the one who comprises within Himself all the attributes of perfection. And that is what is denoted by His words: *"When your Lord took out all their descendants from the loins of the children of Adam and made them testify against themselves"* in that world where they were, asking them who else, if not Him, was their Lord and they replied that He was indeed their Lord.

But when they emerge into this world some of them remember that affirmation and hold to it, becoming believers and affirming the Divine unity; while others – and we seek refuge with Allah from being among them: those predestined to do that – deny it and do not acknowledge either Lordship or Godhood or anything else. They become what people call atheists, not believing in the existence of God or the Divine attributes, forgetting what we all agreed to in that former world when we said we believed and that would affirm Allah's unity and be right-acting.

"Am I not your Lord?" They said, "We testify that indeed You are."

What does *"indeed You are"* mean? It means "Of course You are our Lord." We testified to that against ourselves. We acknowledged

Allah's Lordship and our slavehood, which is its corollary. In that world we accepted Allah's Lordship, which entails all perfection, and accepted our slavehood, which entails all imperfection. But if we want to have a share in perfection we have to apply ourselves to the worship of Allah *ta'ala*. As the Prophet ﷺ told us in the *hadith qudsi* in *Sahih Bukhari*: "My slave continues to draw near to Me through voluntary acts of *'ibada* until I love him; and when I love him I become his hearing with which he hears, his seeing with which he sees, his hand with which he grasps, and his foot with which he walks. If he were to ask Me for something, I would certainly give it to him, and if he sought refuge with me I would certainly grant it to him." If we draw near to our Lord, all good is ours. All good in this world and the Next World lies in drawing near to Allah.

And it is vital for people to appreciate the importance of the Next World, to realise that they are going to die and that they are going to their graves and that, when they are in the grave, their actions will appear to them. If they are right actions they will be a comfort to them; but if they are other than that – and we seek refuge with Allah from it – what will happen then? Their actions will torment them. Right actions will manifest themselves in a delightful form, a beautiful one. The dead person will ask, "Why has Allah honoured me by sending you to me?" It will reply, "I am your right actions. You did me and now I have come to keep you company." But if he has only bad actions to his account, they will appear in a repugnant shape, something horrible to look at, with a foul stench and a hideous appearance, a terrifying apparition. The dead person will say, "Get away from me!" It will reply, "What do you mean get away from you? I am your actions. You're the person who did the bad things which have made me like this." Everyone's actions enter the grave with them, if they are right actions they will be a comfort to them, if they are other than that, they will torment them.

Lest you say on the Day of Rising, 'We knew nothing of this.'

Because on the Day of Rising Allah will question us about the *tawhid* He ordered us to affirm. There will be people who held to that *tawhid* and belief and right action; but there will be others who failed to do that. The people who failed to do it will appeal to Allah saying, "We found our fathers off the path and just followed them." Allah tells us this when He says that they say: *"We found our fathers following a religion and we are simply following in their footsteps."* 43:22 Is that going to do them any good? No, it won't be of any use at all. It will be no good for a Jew to say he is a Jew or for a Christian to say he is a Christian. No. Everyone has been ordered to enter Islam. Allah tells us: *"If anyone desires anything other than Islam as a deen, it will not be accepted from him, and in the Next World he will be among the losers."* 3:84 And again: *"The deen with Allah is Islam."* 3:19 Islam gathers together all good things. It brings together all the actions that bring you closer to Allah and warns you against all the actions which distance you from Allah.

Or lest you say, 'Our forefathers associated others with Allah before our time, and we are merely descendants coming after them.'

In other words we simply followed those before us. For example the Jews at that time, they knew about the existence of Sayyidina

Muhammad, and the existence of the Qur'an and the existence of the *Sunna*, but they preferred what their ancestors followed and refused to follow the path it was now their obligation to follow, and that was the *deen* of Islam. It doesn't matter whether they call themselves Jews or Christians or anything else, everyone who follows anything apart from Islam will be in the Fire. Islam is the only way to go.

But people have to really follow Islam. It can't be just lip service, saying *la ilaha illa'llah, Muhammadun rasulullah*, and then being someone who doesn't do the prayer and indulges in shameful actions, or someone who is subject to pride, envy and rancour. Your Islam has got to be a true Islam. Following Islam and its people means mixing with good people, because your state will be according to the state of the people you are with. If someone who is not very good mixes with good people he himself will become good as well, and if someone who is ignorant mixes with people of knowledge he himself will become knowledgeable and so on.

The Prophet ﷺ told us to keep good company because good company has all good in it. A person will inevitably have a similar state to those he keeps company with. If they are good he will follow them in good and if they are bad he will follow them in their badness. So everyone should choose a companion who obeys Allah, because a follower follows. Young people nowadays, poor things, are in great danger. If they come across good people who attract them to the good then great good will come from them. But if they meet people who corrupt them they will have a hard time in their lives.

Our young people are tremendous, they have fine intellects and great potential, but it is necessary for them to mix with people who will teach them the *deen* and good character. If that happens there will those among them who will support the *deen* and be a great strength to Islam. But if, when they study, they study for the *dunya* alone, just to get some certificate or other. What's the point of that? Your *rizq* is bound to come to you. You should work hard for what will bring you close to Allah, not just work for the *dunya*. In the *dunya* your *rizq* is guaranteed. Even if the whole of the *dunya* was within your grasp, you would still only take from it your allotted *rizq*.

Or lest you say, "Our forefathers associated others with Allah before our time, and we are merely descendants coming after them. So are you going to destroy us for what those purveyors of falsehood did."

They will be destroyed because Allah made things clear to them but then they followed their forefathers in their lack of *deen*, whether they are Jews, Christians, idolaters or fire-worshippers. The main point is that the only thing that will do anybody any good is to enter Islam. *"If anyone desires anything other than Islam as a deen, it will not be accepted from him, and in the akhira he will be among the losers."* 3:84

That is how We make the Signs clear so that hopefully they will return.

This isn't just for the Jews. Allah has also made the Signs clear to us. So that hopefully people will return from a bad state to a good state, from lack of the *deen* to having the *deen*, and from bad behaviour to good behaviour. So a person will move away from bad characteristics, which distance them from Allah, to characteristics which will bring them closer to Allah. The human being has an intellect. Our responsibility for our actions is based on us having intellect. Intellect is what enables us to distinguish between things which are bad and distance us from Allah, so we can abandon them, and things which are good and bring us closer to Allah, so we can adopt them.

Recite to them the tale of him to whom We gave Our Signs,

This is another subject and there is a great lesson in it for our scholars, for our people of knowledge. A scholar, provided he acts on his knowledge, has a high place with Allah. We find the hadith: "The men of knowledge are the inheritors of the Prophets," and there is also another hadith: "If anyone hears two words from a man of knowledge, or eats two mouthfuls with him, or walks two paces with him, Allah will build two cities for him in the Garden, each city twice as big as the whole of this world." So we should honour our men of knowledge and realise what extraordinary people they are and the great benefits we get from them. You only have to eat a mouthful with one or exchange a couple of words or take a step with one, and look what a great gift Allah gives you, a bounty with no limit to it and no end.

but who then casts them to one side,

I seek refuge with Allah! This is a man of knowledge who abandons all the knowledge he has and follows his own whims and desires.

and Shaytan caught up with him. He was one of those lured into error.

The *dunya* came and seduced him, love of power came and seduced him, and bad company came and finished him off. Who is this talking about? It's a man called Ibn Ba'ura. He was a man of knowledge, to such an extent that he was almost a Prophet. But then *dunya* and women came along and seduced him. Then he started making *du'a* against Sayyidina Musa, and that caused the forty years of aimless wandering in the desert for Bani Isra'il, because he had learned the *Ismu'l-Adham*, the Great Name of Allah. Allah had even taught him that *Ismu'l-Adham*. But what good did it do him. They had to spend a long period wandering about aimlessly. And all the while this enemy of Allah had all this knowledge and he also had the *Ismu'l-Adham*. But – and we seek Allah's refuge – in spite of that he cast it aside and followed his whims and desires. The *dunya* deluded him, and its appetites, and its affairs overcame him, and devastated his knowledge.

and Shaytan caught up with him. He was one of those lured into error. And if We had wanted to, We would have raised him up by them.

By those knowledges he had. But the Divine will is over everything. *"If We had wanted to, We would have raised him up by them."* But what was that raising up dependent on? It was dependent on sincere repentance, and doing what Allah ordered him to do and avoiding the things Allah had prohibited for him. But, because of that bad state he was in, Allah consigned him to the Fire – and we seek refuge with Allah from it – where he will stay forever.

But he gravitated towards the earth and pursued his whims and base desires.

Then Allah compares him to a dog.

His metaphor is that of a dog: if you chase it away, it lolls out its tongue and pants, and if you leave it alone, it lolls out its tongue and pants.

Dogs cannot perspire properly. That's why they always pant. Human beings, who can perspire, do not pant like that. But dogs, Allah created them unable to perspire making them have to pant, so: *"if you chase it away, it lolls out its tongue and pants, and if you leave it alone, it lolls out its tongue and pants."* And this is the metaphor Allah uses for this scholar who was stripped of his knowledge and followed his whims and desires. Allah likens him to a dog and then says:

That is the metaphor of those who deny Our Signs.

There you see! This doesn't just apply to this man, it applies to everyone who denies Allah's Signs; and knowledge is necessarily connected to action; anyone who doesn't act according to the knowledge he has, shoving it behind his back, he is also included in this *ayah*.

So tell the story so that hopefully they will reflect.

Tell them the story and make it clear to them what happened to previous communities, about the people who won and the people who lost. So they will follow the way of the winners and avoid the path of the losers.

How evil is the metaphor of those who deny Our Signs. It is themselves that they have badly wronged.

This is because human beings only ever really harm themselves by what they do. If they go out and do bad actions they only harm themselves. They just expose themselves to the loss of this world and the Next. But if Allah takes them by the hand and enables them to use their intellect, they go on the Straight Path. Allah says: *"This is My Path and it is straight, so follow it. Do not follow other ways or you will become cut off from His Way."* 6:154

During Ramadan, for instance, some people just go to cafes or go out for a stroll, whereas the best thing would be to go and do some *rak'ats* or reflect on your wrong actions. This space of Ramadan, Allah has put a great gift in it. I always say it is the storehouse of the year. If someone does a prayer in it, just a *nafila*, it counts as a *fard*. And if he prays a *fard* prayer it counts the same as seventy *fards* at any other time. And not just prayers – every kind of action is multiplied, all good actions count seventy times what they normally do. Dhikr seventy times, fasting seventy times, prayer seventy times, every action is multiplied like that. So if someone has any intellect at all, if they have neglected something outside Ramadan, they will make up for it during Ramadan. Ramadan is the time of making up.

Anyway may Allah give us and you success in gaining good, give us and you love for one another in Allah; and our king, may Allah give him every success, and give him good advisors; and by the baraka of this blessed gathering, may Allah give us joy by the Muslims gaining victory over their enemies, very soon.

7

al-A'raf 7:178-180

مَن يَهْدِ اللَّهُ فَهُوَ الْمُهْتَدِى وَمَن يُضْلِلْ فَأُوْلَٰٓئِكَ هُمُ الْخَٰسِرُونَ ۝

وَلَقَدْ ذَرَأْنَا لِجَهَنَّمَ كَثِيرًا مِّنَ الْجِنِّ وَالْإِنسِ لَهُمْ قُلُوبٌ لَّا يَفْقَهُونَ بِهَا وَلَهُمْ أَعْيُنٌ

لَّا يُبْصِرُونَ بِهَا وَلَهُمْ ءَاذَانٌ لَّا يَسْمَعُونَ بِهَآ أُوْلَٰٓئِكَ كَالْأَنْعَٰمِ بَلْ هُمْ أَضَلُّ

أُوْلَٰٓئِكَ هُمُ الْغَٰفِلُونَ ۝ وَلِلَّهِ الْأَسْمَآءُ الْحُسْنَىٰ فَادْعُوهُ بِهَا وَذَرُوا الَّذِينَ

يُلْحِدُونَ فِىٓ أَسْمَٰٓئِهِ سَيُجْزَوْنَ مَا كَانُوا يَعْمَلُونَ ۝

*Whomever Allah guides is truly guided. But those He
misguides are the lost. We created many of the jinn and
mankind for Hell. They have hearts they do not understand
with. They have eyes they do not see with. They have ears they
do not hear with. Such people are like cattle. No, they are
even further astray! They are the unaware. To Allah belong the
Most Beautiful Names, so call on Him by them and abandon
those who desecrate His Names. They will be repaid for what
they did.*

Allah *'azza wa jall* says in His Mighty Book: *"Whomever Allah
guides is truly guided; but those He misguides are the lost."* We have
already told you that this blessed *surah* is called *Surat al-A'raf*
because Allah mentions in it the people of the *a'raf*, saying: *"And
on the ramparts (a'raf) there will be men."* 7:45 Every *surah* is

named after a word in it. We reached Allah's words: *"Whoever Allah guides is truly guided."* Allah's guidance involves the creation of obedience within the slave, the creation of both obedience and also the strength to carry it out. If we just said the creation of obedience, it could imply that the power to obey comes from the slave. It is the creation of obedience and the power to obey, both of them.

So saying that Allah has guided someone, means that Allah has given them the power to act and then guided them to obedience and worship. Allah has given them the power to perform those acts of worship and obedience to Him. It is all from Him, *subhanah*, both the power and the obedience. *"Whoever Allah guides is truly guided."* There is no doubt that if Allah creates the power to obey in someone and gives him success in doing it, he will certainly live in obedience to Allah *ta'ala*. That's why He says: *"…is truly guided."*

but those He misguides are the lost.

But those who are overtaken by their predestined fate, and whom Allah misguides, we will always find that the reasons for their misguidance are clear. Either they mix with people of low character, who drink alcohol or frequent places of corruption, or make friends with misguided people. If they do that, they too are bound to be misguided. Everything relates back to our Lord but the means must inevitably be there. You don't get misguidance without there being a cause for it.

Allah guides whoever He wills and misguides whoever He wills, but the misguidance will always have a cause. "Why, my son," you may say, "you have got an intellect but still you don't pray and you don't remember Allah, and you don't learn what Allah has made obligatory for you." He may reply, "Allah has not opened the way to guidance for me." Yes He has. He's given him an intellect, He has given him sight, and He has given him the strength to obey Him. The evidence against him will be firmly established.

but those He misguides are the lost.

As we have said, misguidance never comes about without a cause. Allah does not make one of His slaves misguided just like that and make him disobedient or an unbeliever without any cause, there is always a reason for that happening. But the disobedience and disbelief is ascribed to the individual, just as obedience or *taqwa* is, even though the whole business in reality goes back to Allah.

We created many of the jinn and mankind for Hell.

Allah created the Garden and created people for it, making them the inhabitants of the Garden. And He created the Fire and created people for it, and it is only possible for them to be in the Fire. If they entered the Garden it would harm them because Allah created them for Hell. "*We created many of the jinn and mankind for Hell.*" And what brings this about?

They have hearts they do not understand with.

We all have hearts. Allah has given all of us hearts, which we also refer to as our intellects, because heart and intellect are in reality the same thing. The intellect is what we discriminate with, between what is good and what is bad, and between what constitutes obedience and what constitutes disobedience. Those people whose inner sight Allah has opened, and to whom he has given an active intellect, they reflect on things that bring them close to Allah and act on them and they reflect on things that will distance them from Allah and keep away from them. And those who don't do this, it is said of them: *"They have hearts they do not understand with."* Allah has not given them success in reflecting with their hearts. Their hearts are switched off. Their only connection is with *dunya* and its appetites.

They have eyes they do not see with.

About this point the *mufassirun* have something significant to say. They say that Allah *ta'ala* has created this universe and included in it the heavens and the earth and the oceans and the planets and the sun and the moon. All these things must inevitably have a Maker. Are they just going to come about all by themselves? Every made thing necessarily indicates a maker. If you contemplate the universe with all its vastness, you find every part of it perfectly in its place. The heavens don't crash down onto the earth. *"Allah is He Who raised up the heavens without any support,"* (13:2). *"He has made the sun and moon subservient to you, holding steady to their courses, and He has made the night and day subservient to you."* (14:35). Our Lord has made all these things so we should pay attention to what they really show us. Can these things exist without a Maker, without a Bringer-into-being, without a Creator? It's only logical that they must have one. If you don't reflect on these things you have a heart you do not understand with – that doesn't work properly – and eyes that do not really see.

Our intellects, our hearts, are supposed to reflect on these created things, and their incredible variety. *"Among His Signs is the creation of the heavens and earth and the variety of you languages and colours."* (30:21) *"Among His signs is that you see the earth laid bare"* in other words dry *"and then when We send down water on it quivers and swells. He Who gives it life is He Who gives life to the dead."* (41:38) *"Among His Signs are the night and day and the sun and moon. Do not prostrate to the sun nor to the moon. Prostrate to Allah who created them, if you worship Him."* (41:36) If you use your intellect to reflect you are bound to see these created things for what they really are and realise that they must have a Creator. Made things must have a maker. By this means you arrive at the realisation Allah's existence and of the attributes He possesses.

Our Lord, *subhanahu*, has attributes and it is the duty of every person to know them so that his heart becomes conscious of Allah's presence, not oblivious to Him. Our Lord has necessary existence. Our existence, on the other hand, is what? Our existence is conditional. We are exposed to non-existence at any moment, no one can be sure he is safe from annihilation. A man can seem to be in full health and then all of a sudden he is dead. How many people, poor things, I have known who seemed to be healthy and have nothing wrong with them and then suddenly their hearts gave out and they were dead. So the only existence which is necessary and is not subject to non-existence is the existence of Allah, *subhanah*. *"Everyone on it will pass away; but the Face of your Lord will remain, Master of Majesty and Generosity."* (55:24-25) *"All things are passing except His Face."* (28:88)

All this means that the believer should be really vigilant so he will have true understanding. This means being able to reflect because Allah has removed from such a heart the screens which veil it from contemplation and reflection. The tradition goes:

"Reflection for one hour is better than seventy years of worship." And Allah makes it clear that you do not have to look very far: *"And in yourselves as well. Do you not then see?"* (51:21) You were a little drop in your father's loins. Then Allah created sexual desire in your father and so he approached his wife. He simply fulfilled his appetite and went on his way! And the poor woman is the one who got saddled with all the difficulties. Allah tells it to be a drop, then to be a clot, then to be a lump, then to be bones, *"… and clothed the bones in flesh; and then brought him into being as another creature."* (23:14) It is another creature because now it has spirit in it. In all the earlier stages there was still no spirit, not until the bones have been formed. *"…and then brought him into being as another creature. Blessed be Allah, the Best of Creators! Then subsequently you will certainly die. Then on the Day of Rising you will be raised again."* (23:14-16)

There is no escaping resurrection after death. It is inevitable. All of us are going to be raised again. For the human being the first stage of the Next World is the grave; that comes first. We have said that it will either be one of the meadows of the Garden or one of the pits of the Fire. If someone has *taqwa* and goes straight and obeys Allah's commands and avoids His prohibitions, they will be fine. When they get to the grave they will find it to be a beautiful meadow. Allah will open a window for them onto the Garden and Allah will give them angels to keep them company. But if – and we seek refuge with Allah from it – people just spent their time forgetful of Allah, amusing themselves, they will be in a state of terror, terror in their graves, terror at their rising, and terror on the *sirat*. Everyone should grasp the real possibility of this happening.

Anyway Allah says: *"They have hearts they do not understand with. They have eyes they do not see with."* What is the meaning of *"do not see"* here? It means that they do not gain any instruction from their seeing, because when a person truly sees something he gains instruction from it. Instruction comes from reflecting on created things. *"Among His Signs is ... the variety of your languages and colours."* (30:21) All of us come from an identical drop of water and yet one is tall and another short, one white and one black. Who is it who does all this? Allah, *subhanah*. *"Among His Signs is the creation of the heavens and the earth and the variety of your languages and colours."* (30:21) We are all from an identical drop so we should all be the same, we should all look the same, and all be the same colour but all this variation occurs. Why? Because it is the will of our Master that we should be different in order that we can know Allah.

If someone asks how come, when all of us are from a tiny drop, this one is white and that one black, this one short and that one tall, the answer is that this indicates that Allah our Lord, *subhanah*, has effective Power, and that He has defining Will, and that He has perfecting Wisdom. Nothing appears in this world which was not known in advance, defined by will, brought about by power, and designed by wisdom. This is what the people of knowledge say. Everything in this world was known in advance; this gathering of ours was fore-known, and then will defined its size, then power made it happen, in other words brought us together. Everything in existence can only come about by going through these stages. Divine Knowledge fore-knows it, Divine Will defines it, Divine Power brings it out, and Divine Wisdom designs it. These are all attributes of Allah.

They have eyes they do not see with.

"See" meaning gain instruction. As Allah says elsewhere: *"People of insight, take note!"* (59:2) A person sees these created things and gains instruction. Who decides what happens in this world, and about the creatures in it, their different forms and colours and livelihoods and their thoughts and whisperings. All those things: *"...and the whole affair is returned to Him."* (11:121)

They have ears they do not hear with.

Their ears are of no use to them. Although they listen it is just as if they had no hearing at all. They only hear ugly things which distance them from Allah. If you want light in your hearing you have to protect it. You have to understand that the hearer is partner in what he hears. For instance, if there is a group of people gossiping and you are sitting with them, don't take part in any backbiting or you will be with them on the Day of Rising. Either get up and go or stop them doing it. You might say, "Look, my friends, this is Ramadan. It's obligatory for us to guard our tongues and backbiting actually breaks the fast. We must guard our eyes and guard our ears and guard our tongues so our fast will be safe and correct. We ruin it by backbiting and slander and keeping bad company."

This is because the company you keep determines the state you are in. You will be judged for what happens while you are sitting with them. You can't say I just happened to be sitting with them. No, their guilt will also include you. There are people who have *taqwa* and fear Allah but don't control their tongues and are then overpowered by bad action. *"Be fearful of trials which will not afflict solely those among you who do wrong."* (8:25) This person we are talking about who has fear of Allah goes and sits with some people and, when they start backbiting in front of him, doesn't say anything, he participates in the wrong the other people are doing. He is included as well.

Such people are like cattle.

The word "cattle" includes camels, cows and sheep. People like this will in fact find that cows and sheep are better than them because the animals know what is good for them and act on it, whereas these people know what is good for them and then do nothing about it. The animals know what is good for them and act on it. An animal will not eat any kind of plant which is going to harm it, or see a cliff and fall over it, or see a beast of prey which could kill it and then go near it. It is clear that animals manage their affairs in a way which is good for them. But human beings, for all their intellect and their hearts, see things which are bound to destroy them and goes straight for them. Therefore, the animal is better than him.

Such people are like cattle. No, they are even further astray!

Further astray than animals! If a human being, who has an intellect, gets involved with things which distance him from Allah, cows and camels and sheep are better than him. The animals know what is good for them and act on that, whereas people like this know what is good for them and then do the opposite. They know that if they disobey Allah they will be punished but they still go on and disobey Allah. They know that *haram* things will distance them from Allah and yet they fall into the *haram*. What is the result? The animals are better than them.

134

They are the unaware.

What has brought about this disaster? Unawareness of Allah. Imam Junayd wrote about wrong action and said that the worst wrong action he knew was forgetfulness of our generous Lord. *"He Who created you and formed you and proportioned you and assembled you in whatever way He willed."* (82:7-8) If you put all the wrong actions on one side and then put unawareness of Allah on the other, it will prove greater than all of them. He is the One who is being good to you every second and with every breath you take, so how is it possible for you to be unmindful of him. You should always be saying *"Al-hamdulillahi wa shukru lillah"* and always be saying *"la ilaha ill'llah"* and always be saying *"Allahumma salli 'ala Sayyidina Muhammad"*; you should always be remembering Allah.

Allah instructs us, saying: *"...remember Allah standing, sitting and lying on your sides."* (4:102) Allah has left us no time or state in which to be unaware of Him. *"...remember Allah standing, sitting and lying on your sides."* 4:102 And the hadith has come: "No people gather in a house to remember Allah without the angels surrounding them, and mercy covering them, and Allah mentioning them to those who are with Him." That *"la ilaha illa llah"* you say finds its place under Allah's throne. The *dhikr* you do all takes on forms, beautiful forms, which gather under the throne and worship and then Allah writes the reward for the people doing the *dhikr*, who have gathered together to remember Him.

The only way to banish shaytan from your presence is *dhikr* of Allah. As Allah says: *"If someone shuts his eyes to the remembrance of the All-Merciful, We assign him a shaytan who becomes his bosom friend – they debar them from the path, yet they still think they are guided."* (43:35-36) A person should not turn to other than his Lord. Why should you put yourself in danger. Sometimes say *"astaghfirullah"*, sometimes *"allahumma salli ala Sayyidina Muhammad"*, sometimes *"la ilaha illa"llah"* and sometimes *"al-hamdu lillahi wa shukru lillah"*, so that you are always remembering Allah. Allah tells us: *"Only in the remembrance of Allah can the heart find peace."* (13:29)

Your heart will have no peace, will not be with its Lord, except if you remember Allah. *"Only in the remembrance of Allah can the heart find peace."* (13:29) If you remember Allah you won't any more be subject to seeing nothing but this world and being anxious about it, because our Lord will give you contentment and tranquillity in your heart. Your heart, my friend, will no longer be obsessed with just this world and its appetites. If someone remembers Allah this world leaves his heart and love of Allah enters it and he forgets everything else. Our Lord says: *"Only in the remembrance of Allah can the heart find peace."* (13:29)

To Allah belong the Most Beautiful Names, so call on Him by them.

As well as commanding us to do *dhikr* of Him, Allah has also given us Names to do it with. These Names of Allah are ninety-nine in number. It has been said: "Allah has ninety-nine Names and whoever enumerates them enters the Garden." In other words whoever memorises them and knows their meanings. What will happen to him? He will enter the Garden, in this world and the Next. In this world he will roam freely in their meanings. In His Name the Most Merciful, in His Name the Almighty, His Name the Ever-Returning, His Name the All-Powerful – they are all Names of our Lord and He has given them special qualities. For every Name there is a secret in its number and a particular quality in its meaning.

If you are going to do *dhikr* with a particular Name, you must know its meaning and the number of times you should repeat it. And if someone does a lot of *dhikr* and it gets too much for him to manage, he can do it sixty-six times which is the number of the Name Allah. Because the letters of the Name "Allah" add up to sixty-six. The people of knowledge say that if someone has a *dhikr* and it gets too much for him to manage he can reduce it to sixty-six. Then that sixty-six will take the place of the larger number.

Anyway they say that for every Name there is a secret in its number and a particular quality in its meaning. For instance the name *"al-Latif"*. This *Latif* is one of the Names of Allah and those who do dhikr with it do it 129 times. If you want you can do it after each *fard* prayer. Allah protects those who do it so that if something bad happens He protects them from it. I know quite a lot of people who do it and they do it this number of times. 129 times.

And what is the meaning of *al-Latif.* It signifies the One who expedites good things for you and keeps every bad thing away from you. The One who brings close to you all good things and distances all bad things from you. That's the approximate meaning of it. So when you say *"ya Latif"* it is as if you are saying "O my Lord keep all bad away from me and bring all good things close." This Name brings all good things close and keeps away everything that causes a person harm.

and abandon those who desecrate His Names.

Those who give them no weight. But Allah *subhanah* mentions these Names in His Book. His Name *al-Qadir, al-Aziz, ar-Rahman, ar-Rahim, at-Tawwab* and so on; all of them are mentioned in the Qur'an. All these 99 names are in the Qur'an, delineated with truth. We find *Qadir, Nasir,* and *Tawwab* and there is *Rahim* there and *Rahman* and *'Aziz,* and all the other Names, and all of them, of course, refer back to Allah.

"To Allah belong the Most Beautiful Names, so call on Him by them." In other words connect yourself to Him through them, and this is done by saying them the right number of times. But if that number gets too much for you, you can reduce it to sixty-six. Because regarding this the people of knowledge have said that if the number relating to a name is too many for someone, they can reduce it to sixty-six, which is the number of the *ismu'l-mufrad.* There is sixty-six in it: the *alif* is one the *lam* is thirty and the second *lam* is thirty and the *ha* is five. How many is that altogether? Sixty-six. For *astaghfirullah* you can do sixty-six when its true number is 200 or 3000. And the Prayer on the Prophet, whose number is 1000 or 8000, also sixty-six and so on.

As we have said a person's heart will never be at peace, and Shaytan will never leave him, and his state with his Lord will never be put right, except by *dhikr* of Allah. That's why Allah says to us: *"Do not be one of the unaware."* (7:205) And as we also said the greatest disaster for any human being is to be unaware of Allah's presence. How is it possible, when Allah *subanah* says He has: *"...showered His blessings upon you, both outwardly and inwardly"* (31:19), that you can be unmindful of Him. You must always be saying *"al-hamdulillah"* always *"la ilaha illa'llah"* always *"allahumma salli ala Sayyidina Muhammad"*. But frequently people's tongues are not doing that. So in your work or when you are travelling or walking to some place, wake your heart up and say to yourself, "Why don't you say *astaghfirullah* or *la ilaha illa'llah* or *allahumma salli ala Sayyidina Muhammad*." I'll leave it there today.

May Allah give us and you success in performing good actions; and make us and you people who love one another in Allah; and seal our lives and yours with the happiness which Allah has reserved for His *awliya*; and make the best and happiest days of our lives the day we meet Him; and make *du'a* for me this Ramadan, that I remain with you; I am not well but such is old age!

Surat al-An'am

6:1-31

8

al-An'am 6:1-3

الْحَمْدُ لِلَّهِ الَّذِي خَلَقَ السَّمَوَاتِ وَالْأَرْضَ وَجَعَلَ الظُّلُمَاتِ وَالنُّورَ ثُمَّ الَّذِينَ كَفَرُوا
بِرَبِّهِمْ يَعْدِلُونَ ۝ هُوَ الَّذِي خَلَقَكُمْ مِنْ طِينٍ ثُمَّ قَضَى أَجَلًا وَأَجَلٌ مُسَمًّى
عِنْدَهُ ثُمَّ أَنْتُمْ تَمْتَرُونَ ۝ وَهُوَ اللَّهُ فِي السَّمَوَاتِ وَفِي الْأَرْضِ يَعْلَمُ سِرَّكُمْ
وَجَهْرَكُمْ وَيَعْلَمُ مَا تَكْسِبُونَ ۝

Praise belongs to Allah Who created the heavens and the earth
and appointed darkness and light. Then those who disbelieve
make others equal to their Lord! It is He Who created you from
clay and then decreed a fixed term, and another fixed term is
specified with Him. Yet you still have doubts! He is Allah in
the heavens and in the earth. He knows what you keep secret
and what you make public. (6:1-3)

Allah, *azza wa jalla*, says in His Mighty Book: "*In the name of*
Allah the All-Merciful, the Most Merciful. Praise belongs to Allah
who created the heavens and the earth and appointed darkness and
light." This *surah* is called *Surat al-An'am*. It is called *Surat al-*
An'am because in it Allah *ta'ala* mentions *al-an'am* – livestock:
"*And also animals (al-an'am) for riding and for haulage and animals*
for slaughtering and for wool." (6:143) Every *surah* of the Qur'an
is named after a word in it and for that reason it is called *Surat*

al-An'am. It contains one hundred and sixty *ayahs* all of which came down in Makka except for a few *ayahs* which came down in Madina.

In the Name of Allah the All-Merciful, Most Merciful.

Every *surah* begins with the *basmalah*. "*In the Name of Allah the All-Merciful, Most Merciful.*" And they say about the *basmalah*, that the nearness of it to the *ismu'l-'adhm*, is the same as the nearness of the iris to the pupil in the eye. Anyone who perseveres in its *dhikr* will always be protected. Why is that? It is because there are nineteen letters in it and that is the number of the *zabaniyya* angels of Jahannam. So if someone perseveres with it Allah rescues him from the *zabaniyya* of Jahannam. When you say *bismillah* before you do something, you are saying: "I eat or I drink or I sleep or I recite or I write in the Name of Allah the All-Merciful, Most Merciful." What is its meaning, its secret? You are saying in the name of Allah, thus indicating the essence, the essence of *Mawlana*.

Allah has many Names: "*To Allah belong the most beautiful Names*", but the greatest of His Names is this Name, the Name Allah. It is the greatest name and the Sufis and other than them are in agreement about this. The name Allah contains all the other names. The name *ar-Rahman*: its meaning is the One who bestows great blessings, the great general blessings such as Islam and *iman* and good health and other such things. This is the area covered by the name *ar-Rahman*. However, there are also particularised blessings such as a person's nails which they need in order to scratch with and to pick up tiny things, or the eyelashes, which protect the eyes from dust, and the eyebrows which stop sweat getting into the eyes. All these things, which are known as particularised blessings, are in the realm of the Name *ar-Rahim*. This is the area covered by the name *ar-Rahim*.

It is said that the saying of *bismillahi'r-rahmani'r-raheem* has the same standing as the *ismu'l-'adhm* and everyone should persevere in saying it. When someone enters his house they should say: "I seek refuge with Allah from the accursed Shaytan, in the name of Allah the All-Merciful Most Merciful" then Shaytan won't enter with them or any other bad thing. And Allah will bless their food for them when they say it before eating. When a person starts to eat they should always say *bismillah*, or even better *bismillahi'r-rahmani'r-rahim*.

Praise be to Allah

This praise is lauding Allah for the immense and majestic attributes He possesses. We praise Him by describing Him by any of His beautiful attributes and Allah loves it when His beautiful attributes are mentioned. There are many Prophetic hadiths that indicate that the person who praises *Sidi Rabbi* has high standing with Him. He, *subhanah*, loves to be praised and lauded. But we must remember that it is He Who creates this praise in us. There are two aspects to this. There is that of being the means of the praise taking place, which we link to ourselves, and then there is the reality, which is that it is Allah who creates that praise we praise Him with in us and He creates it in us, Himself. When you say *al-hamdulillah*, He is the one who creates that praise in you, your very saying of the words *al-hamdulillah*. Allah says: "*Praise be to Allah...*" that means every kind of praise and every beautiful characteristic, every praiseworthy attribute, all of those belong to Allah, they all are possessed by Allah.

Who created the heavens and the earth

He *subhanah* has created everything and He started with the creation of the heavens and earth. We can see the heavens: the sun, the moon and the stars and the rain that comes down from it. All those things are indications of His power, the power of Allah, the pin-pointing, the specification, of His will, and the perfection of His wisdom, and the all-embracing nature of His knowledge. When Allah tells us to look at the heavens, we see they are raised without any pillars or supports. He has placed amazing things, such as the vast constellations, in them indicating his Immensity, *subhanah*. And there are angels subservient to His command. There is no heaven which does not have myriads of angels in it; among them are those who are bowing and never stand up straight; among them are those who are prostrating and never get to raise their heads; among them are those who are standing and never bend; each one of them has their own specific form of worship. There is not one inch of space where there is not an angel bowing or prostrating or glorifying their Lord.

and appointed darkness and light

Every kind of darkness whether in the sensory or the meaning. And He has also created light, every kind of light. There is the light of the human being, which comes from himself, and separate lights, like the sun and moon and stars; all those things give out light. *Mawlana* gives them light at every moment. The question is whether a person, when they see the immense power of our Lord, *subhanah*, and these indications, which point to His existence and the existence of His attributes, whether they believe or disbelieve. They should believe in Allah and worship Him and not associate anything with Him, not associate anything else with Him whatsoever.

When this *surah* came down it came down accompanied by seventy thousand angels, seventy thousand angels. And when it came down the Prophet ﷺ prostrated to Allah. A great deal has come down to us regarding its benefits. It has been said that Allah gives the reward of seventy thousand angels to anyone who recites it. In fact it is only necessary to recite three *ayahs* because this *surah* is quite long and to recite all of it would be difficult. So there are three *ayahs* in it which give this great reward: from the beginning as far as the word "*taksibun*". Recitation of these first three *ayahs* give this tremendous reward. "*Praise belongs to Allah who created the heavens and the earth and appointed darkness and light. Then those who disbelieve make others equal to their Lord! It is He Who created you from clay and then decreed a fixed term, and another fixed term is specified with Him. Yet you still have doubts! He is Allah in the heavens and in the earth. He knows what you keep secret and what you make public and He knows what you earn.*" Up to there.

If someone recites these *ayahs* Allah assigns to him angels that protect him and stop Shaytan getting near him. He has seventy thousand angels looking after him and some of these angels have weapons and if a *shaytan* gets near him an angel whacks him with one of these weapons! In any case everyone should learn this passage by heart and use it. It is only three *ayahs* long: "*Praise belongs to Allah who created the heavens and the earth and appointed darkness and light. Then those who are kafir make others equal to their Lord! It is He Who created you from clay and then decreed a fixed term, and another fixed term is specified with Him. Yet you still have doubts! He is Allah in the heavens and in the earth. He knows what you keep secret and what you make public and He knows what you earn."*

These *ayahs* are accompanied by seventy thousand angels and give protection from every kind of danger. So when someone gets up or wants to go to sleep at night he should recite them. Then he will be protected both during the night and the day.

Then those who are kafir make others equal to their Lord.

They see these things which only Allah is able to do, only Allah, yet in spite of that they worship idols and statues, which don't bring any benefit or any harm. Such people have no intellect at all. They make these idols and paint these pictures and then begin to worship them and think it benefits or harms them, whereas Allah *subhanahu wa ta'la* is the Creator of everything. *'Then those who disbelieve make others equal to their Lord.'* They equate the worship of Allah with the worship of other than Him, in other words idols. They equate worshipping Allah, who alone is entitled to be worshipped, with the worship of idols and objects, which they worship apart from Allah.

It is He Who created you from clay

This refers to Sayyidina Adam, because Allah created Sayyidina Adam from clay. When Allah desired to create him he sent Jibril to collect clay from every corner of the earth. But wherever he went the earth said, 'Not from here! I don't want the soil from here to be used for creating anyone.' So he shied away from it and left. Then Mika'il came as well but once again the earth was reluctant to give up any clay, saying, 'This Adam is going to be disobedient to Allah and I do not want my clay to play any part in his creation.' It begged Allah not to take anything from it but then the angel of death arrived – and you don't mess about with him! – the earth tried to plead with him but he said 'Allah has given me an order and I must carry that order out.' And he took earth of different colours from here and there. Then Allah gathered all that clay together and synthesized it and created from it Sayyidina Adam, *alayhi salam*. He was a creature made of earth.

So the creation of all of us reverts back to clay because all of us are descendants of Sayyidina Adam and he was created from clay. But Allah created all of us from a drop. What is the *ayah*? Allah created Sayyidina Adam from clay, there's no confusion about that, and He created us from a drop. *"We created man from the purest kind of clay; then made him a drop in a secure receptacle; then formed the drop into a clot and formed the clot into a lump and formed the lump into bones and clothed the bones in flesh; and then brought him into being as another creature. Blessed be Allah, the Best of Creators! Then subsequently you will certainly die. Then on the Day of Rising you will be raised again."* (23:12-16) This passage from *Surat al-Muminun* is the one I meant.

This gives the details of the whole process. *"From the purest kind of clay; then made him* – not Adam himself but his descendants – *a drop in a secure receptacle;"* So Adam was created from pure clay and his descendants from a drop. And the *"secure receptacle"* is the woman's womb. That drop comes when a man gets into a certain state and has sexual intercourse with his wife; then the drop starts to develop. Allah says be a drop and after forty days be a clot

149

then after forty days be a lump then after that it becomes bones. Then Allah clothes it. Then Allah makes him 'another creature' by breathing the *ruh* into it.

So Sayyidina Adam was created from earth and we are created from that drop. Every one of us has an allotted time. *"When their time comes they cannot delay it a single hour or bring it forward."* 7:32 The fixed term is in fact unknown to us, not something clear. Some people die young, some middle-aged and some old. This is so that there is always a state of fear. No one should feel secure about this matter. You have to keep on your toes. As the saying goes: "When you reach the evening do not expect to last to the morning and when you reach the morning do not expect to see the night." You do not know what is going to happen to you. It is Allah, glory be to Him, who governs you by His Will.

In any case we human beings are left in the dark about this matter so we will remain between hope and fear. Allah has not told us the time we are going to die. So that sometimes we hope for His mercy and other times we fear His punishment. If we see His mercy we have hope and if we see His punishment we have fear because Allah possess both majesty and beauty. So the slave should always be between hope and fear.

It is He Who created you from clay and then decreed a fixed term. Yet you still have doubts!

We don't know what the fixed term with Him is. We know about our lives so far, don't you understand, but there is a fixed term with Allah that no one knows. Some people die young, some middle-aged, some old. No one can feel safe.

Yet you still have doubts.

You have doubts about Lordship, whether the Lord exists or not. Our Lord is the One Who creates, provides for you, gives to you and withholds from you and gives everyone a known lifespan which they cannot exceed. When that fixed term comes nothing can prevent death coming. Death is inevitable. No matter how long you live, you are still going to die. Maybe you will live to a hundred and die, maybe 120, maybe 140, the outside limit for a man's life is 160 years. But ideally no more than 120, because up to that time he is fine but once he exceeds 120 he has no strength left; his strength leaves him completely. We should have recourse to the *du'a*: "O Allah, keep me alive as long as You deem life to be good for me and let me die when You deem death to be better for me." And "Make life an increase for me in all good things and make death a respite for me from all bad things."

Death can have a thousand blessings in it. If you reflect you will see that death can contain a thousand blessings. Because every sinew of your body is potentially exposed to illnesses. When you die you are relieved from all illness and disease. Then there are the obligations of the *shari'a* which you have to fulfil. When you die you have no more obligations at all. Because we have many such obligations. Death is the end of your obligations and the end of the illnesses you are afraid of. And likewise bad company, people who are no good for us, we are rid of them for good. So death can have a thousand mercies in it. People find it difficult but there is a great mercy in it. "Death is a gift to every believer."

He is Allah in the heavens and in the earth

Meaning He is worshipped in the heavens and worshipped on

earth. Worshipped in the heavens because the angels are charged with worship. *"They glorify Him by night and day without ever flagging."* (21:20) And on earth by us creatures: both jinn and humans. Us on earth and the angels in the heavens. They are all worshipping Allah, glory to Him.

He knows what you keep secret and what you make public.

He knows what you keep secret. Nothing in your heart is hidden from Him. *"He knows the eyes' deceit and what people's breasts conceal."* (40:19) *"We know what his own self whispers to him. We are nearer to him than his jugular vein."* (50:16) He is always scrutinizing our innermost secrets, so anyone who is truly aware of what this means, how could they possibly disobey Allah? Anyone who really knows Allah is watching them and sees the innermost secrets of their heart and everything they do with their limbs outwardly will certainly be afraid of Allah. They will say: "If I fall into something forbidden, firstly I may well get some punishment in this world and in the Next World it is guaranteed. So I am fearful that Allah will join the punishment of this life and the Next for me." As He tells us, *subhanah*: *"Any disaster that strikes you is through what your own hands have earned and He pardons much."* (42:28) If a human being makes some mistake he exposes himself to ruin. But our Lord, glory to Him, pardons us and excuses us. And if we do fall into some wrong action then He accepts our repentance.

He knows what you keep secret and what you make public and He knows what you earn.

All right, let's leave it there for the moment. We were talking about

Ramadan. If someone is ill – this is a question someone asked – if someone is ill, should they put up with the hardship and fast or should they break the fast? And likewise travellers, if they are healthy should they fast or not? Allah says: *"But any of you who are ill or on a journey should fast a number of other days."* (2:183) People who are ill should not make things difficult for themselves; no, they should break their fast. And it is even the case that if they do fast, that fast of theirs is not valid. Because Allah told them to fast a *"number of other days."* They are refusing to accept a mercy Allah has granted them. People who are strict on this point say that if a person fasts when they are ill then their fast is invalid, because Allah says: "Do not fast when you are ill."

And the same applies when someone is traveling, they should break the fast and eat. Even if they are healthy. Allah says: *"a number of other days."* There is man who is ill, poor fellow, and can scarcely stand up and then he begins to fast. His fast may not even be acceptable. If we tread the path the Companions trod, they all took the *ayah* according to its obvious meaning: *"a number of other days."* Allah does not impose the fast on someone who is ill and does not impose it on a traveller when he is traveling. He says: "Wait until you are well" and "Wait until you reach your home," then you make up whatever you missed of Ramadan. Anyway you should make sure you are aware of this matter.

9

al-An'am 6:4-13

وَمَا تَأْتِيهِم مِّنْ ءَايَةٍ مِّنْ ءَايَتِ رَبِّهِمْ إِلَّا كَانُواْ عَنْهَا مُعْرِضِينَ ۝ فَقَدْ كَذَّبُواْ بِالْحَقِّ
لَمَّا جَآءَهُمْ فَسَوْفَ يَأْتِيهِمْ أَنۢبَٰٓؤُاْ مَا كَانُواْ بِهِۦ يَسْتَهْزِءُونَ ۝ أَلَمْ يَرَوْاْ كَمْ أَهْلَكْنَا مِن
قَبْلِهِم مِّن قَرْنٍ مَّكَّنَّٰهُمْ فِى ٱلْأَرْضِ مَا لَمْ نُمَكِّن لَّكُمْ وَأَرْسَلْنَا ٱلسَّمَآءَ عَلَيْهِم مِّدْرَارًا
وَجَعَلْنَا ٱلْأَنْهَٰرَ تَجْرِى مِن تَحْتِهِمْ فَأَهْلَكْنَٰهُم بِذُنُوبِهِمْ وَأَنشَأْنَا مِنۢ بَعْدِهِمْ
قَرْنًا ءَاخَرِينَ ۝ وَلَوْ نَزَّلْنَا عَلَيْكَ كِتَٰبًا فِى قِرْطَاسٍ فَلَمَسُوهُ بِأَيْدِيهِمْ لَقَالَ ٱلَّذِينَ
كَفَرُوٓاْ إِنْ هَٰذَآ إِلَّا سِحْرٌ مُّبِينٌ ۝ وَقَالُواْ لَوْلَآ أُنزِلَ عَلَيْهِ مَلَكٌ
وَلَوْ أَنزَلْنَا مَلَكًا لَّقُضِىَ ٱلْأَمْرُ ثُمَّ لَا يُنظَرُونَ ۝ وَلَوْ جَعَلْنَٰهُ مَلَكًا
لَّجَعَلْنَٰهُ رَجُلًا وَلَلَبَسْنَا عَلَيْهِم مَّا يَلْبِسُونَ ۝ وَلَقَدِ ٱسْتُهْزِئَ
بِرُسُلٍ مِّن قَبْلِكَ فَحَاقَ بِٱلَّذِينَ سَخِرُواْ مِنْهُم مَّا كَانُواْ بِهِۦ
يَسْتَهْزِءُونَ ۝ قُلْ سِيرُواْ فِى ٱلْأَرْضِ ثُمَّ ٱنظُرُواْ كَيْفَ كَانَ
عَٰقِبَةُ ٱلْمُكَذِّبِينَ ۝ قُل لِّمَن مَّا فِى ٱلسَّمَٰوَٰتِ وَٱلْأَرْضِ قُل لِّلَّهِ كَتَبَ
عَلَىٰ نَفْسِهِ ٱلرَّحْمَةَ لَيَجْمَعَنَّكُمْ إِلَىٰ يَوْمِ ٱلْقِيَٰمَةِ لَا رَيْبَ فِيهِ

*Not one of their Lord's signs comes to them without their
turning away from it. They deny the truth each time it comes
to them but news of what they were mocking will certainly
reach them. Have they not seen how many generations We*

destroyed before them which We had established on the earth far more firmly than We have established you? We sent down heaven upon them in abundant rain and made rivers flow under them but we destroyed them for their wrong actions and raised up further generations after them. Even if We were to send down a book to you on parchment pages and they were actually to touch it with their own hands those who disbelieve would still say, "This is nothing but downright magic." They say, "Why has an angel not been sent down to him?" If We were to send down an angel, that would be the end of the affair and they would have no reprieve. And if We had made him an angel We would still have made him a man, and further confused for them, the very thing they are confused about! Messengers before you were also mocked but those who jeered were engulfed by what they mocked. Say: "Travel about the earth and see the final fate of the deniers." Say: "To whom does everything in the heavens and earth belong?" Say: "To Allah." He has made mercy incumbent on Himself. He will gather you to the Day of Rising about which there is no doubt. (6:5- 13)

As we have already mentioned this *surah* is called *Suratu'l-An'am* because, as we have also said, every *surah* is named after a word from it and Allah mentions *al-an'am* in it: *"And also animals (al-an'am) for riding and for haulage..."* as will come later in this *surah*. It speaks about livestock animals. It has 160 or so *ayahs* in it. This *surah* was sent down to the Prophet ﷺ in *Makka al-Mukarrama* and it came down at night in one go. And there were very few *surahs* which came down in one go. But this one did and arrived with a whole host of angels with a tremendous thundering of glorification and unification. They came at night and the Prophet ﷺ got up and faced those angels and began to prostrate saying, *'Subhana rabbi'l-adhim'* because of what he saw of the power of those angels who descended with glorification and unification and exaltation. And this *surah* contains great *ayahs* indicating the unity of Allah and the perfections He possesses. That's why it encompasses all the virtues.

It begins with praise in its first *ayah*: *"Praise belongs to Allah who created the Heavens and the earth and appointed darkness and light. Then those who disbelieve make others equal to their Lord."* It was addressed to the people of Makka because the people of Makka used to worship statues and idols and they were bent on worshipping them. They didn't have confidence in anything else. When the Prophet ﷺ came with what he came with they completely rejected him, despite the fact that they knew his worth as they used to call him *al-Amin*, the Trustworthy. But when he came with Prophethood and the Message they totally denied him, sometimes calling him a magician and sometime a soothsayer, sometimes saying someone was instructing him and things like that. Very few of them submitted, became Muslim, until after the conquest of Makka when he said to them, "Go, you are free."

In spite of all the trouble they had given him he never held it against them ﷺ. They said, "Pardon us, Allah loves the good-doers." That was after they had made things so difficult for him and his Companions. He entered Makka and they were assembled in front of him and he said to them, "What do you think I am going to do with you?" They said, "You are a noble brother and a noble nephew." He said, "Go, you are free." Go away and do whatever you like. He didn't tell them to become Muslims or to stay there. They started to reflect and become Muslim of their own accord. And all of that came about because of his noble character ﷺ and his great forgiving nature.

And we reached His words, may He be exalted: "*Not one of their Lord's signs comes to them,*" to the people of Makka, O Muhammad, "*without their turning away from it.*" When any Qur'anic *ayah* arrived, he would say this has been revealed to me and this is its reward and this is its meaning, but they didn't believe him and said this is just soothsaying or myths of earlier peoples and things like that.

They deny the truth each time it comes to them.

What is the truth referred to here? It is the Qur'an. The Qur'an is the Truth itself. The Qur'an is all truth from beginning to end. So he used to recite the Qur'an to them and they listened to it and they knew it was the word of Allah. But *kufr* – and we seek refuge with Allah from it – had taken firm hold of them and love of idols and statues. And afterwards most of those who became Muslim only did so after the Conquest of Makka.

But news of what they were mocking will certainly reach them.

The news will soon reach those who rejected him both in this life and the Next. As regards this world, it happened at the Battle of Badr; all those who cursed the Prophet ﷺ were all killed, every last one of them. Allah *ta'ala* gave him a free hand over the idolaters and many were killed. Some of them were captured and were imprisoned and some died. Allah gave him a free hand over all of them.

Have they not seen how many generations we destroyed before them which We had established on the earth far more firmly than We have established you?

Allah, *tabaraka wa ta'ala*, is telling them to reflect on the previous Prophets and past centuries and to look at those people who did not believe in their Messengers, what happened to them and what Allah did to them. He says: *"We seized each one of them for their wrong actions. Against some We sent a sudden squall of stones; some of them were seized by the Great Blast; some We caused the earth to swallow up; and some We drowned; Allah did not wrong them; rather they wronged themselves."* (29:40) *"rather they wronged themselves."* Reflect on the past peoples who denied their Prophets and Messengers, what befell them and how Allah dealt with them. It is made clear to us. *"We seized each one of them for their wrong actions."* The truth is that their destruction is guaranteed; Allah destroyed all of them. *"Against some We sent a sudden squall of stones; some of them were seized by the Great Blast; some We caused the earth to swallow up; and some We drowned; Allah did not wrong them; rather they wronged themselves."* (29:40)

We sent down heaven upon them in abundant rain and made rivers flow under them. But we destroyed them for their wrong actions.

Allah destroyed them for their wrong actions. But not until He had bestowed enormous blessings on them. Some of them were at the very limit of what it is possible to be blessed with, when their Messenger came to them, like the people of Sayyidina Nuh or the people of Sayyidina Hud or the people of Sayyidina Salih. All the Prophets, none of them were believed at first; their people never came to them straightaway and said we believe in you. There was no Prophet who was not rejected. *"Messengers before you were also denied."* (6:35) It wasn't only him ﷺ who was denied. Only a few people ever believed.

But we destroyed them for their wrong actions and raised up further generations after them.

So Allah destroyed that people and another people came along. We have the people of Hud and the people of Shu'ayb and other peoples. To each of them a Prophet would come accompanied by miracles and other signs and they would reject them; their own families would reject them and their neighbours and relatives and tribe; they all rejected them. Very few would believe. Allah tells us: *"But those who believed with him were only few."* (11:40)

Even if We were to send down a book to you on parchment pages and they were actually to touch it with their own hands.

They still wouldn't believe. Now these people, these idolaters of Makka, said to him "Bring us some angel or make some book come down to us from heaven." They weren't persuaded, by his recitation of the Qur'an to them, that Jibril had brought it down and that he was reciting the Book of Allah to them. They said, "No, we need to see an angel and for an actual physical book to be sent down to you which can be read out to us so we can hear it." Allah *ta'ala* referred to that in this *ayah*. They wanted a book to come from heaven to them that they could touch and see. But what would they say if it did?

Those who disbelieve would still say, "This is nothing but downright magic."

This just shows their state of denial, those enemies of Allah.

They say, "Why has an angel not been sent down to him?"

This is what we were just talking about. If a book had been sent down they still wouldn't have been satisfied with it. So what did they ask for then, an angel. But what would happen if an angel did come down? It would destroy them. They hadn't got the necessary capacity to either see it or relate to it. That is why Allah continues:

If We were to send down an angel, that would be the end of the affair and they would have no reprieve.

If an angel did come down and they still didn't believe they would all have been destroyed on the spot, they would all have been completely wiped out. Even if an angel had come down and they had not believed it. So Allah says about that: *they would have no reprieve.* Their destruction would not be delayed an instant. If an angel had come down and said, "He is a Messenger and I am an angel," and then they did not confirm that, they would have exposed themselves immediately to total destruction.

And if We had made him an angel

Supposing that happened, they would not know how to deal with it anyway. Allah says: *"And if We had made him an angel We would still have made him a man, and further confused for them, the very thing they are confused about!"* Like when Jibril ﷺ actually did come. When he came to the Prophet he came in a human form, in the form of a man, he didn't come in his own tremendous form.

160

He has six hundred wings, each wing spanning between east and west. No he came in the form of a man.

and further confused for them, the very thing they are confused about.

So it might well be that they wouldn't believe it was an angel even if one did come. They would just say it wasn't an angel anyway.

Messengers before you were also mocked.

This is addressed to the Prophet 🌸. Allah is telling him: "There has never been a Prophet who was not mocked by his people, it is not just you." *"So be steadfast as the Messengers with firm resolve were also steadfast."* (46:35) Do not be impatient. Allah is bound to support you. But you must have patience, tremendous patience. Then when Allah wanted to help him 🌸, He ordered him to emigrate to Madina and his position became very strong and then he came back to Makka as a conqueror, and at the same time gave them safe passage.

But those who jeered were engulfed by what they mocked.

But those who used to mock the Prophets were all destroyed. *"We seized each one of them for their wrong actions."* All who mocked and denied the Messengers, what was done to them? *"We seized each one of them for their wrong actions. Against some We sent a sudden squall of stones; some of them were seized by the Great Blast; some We caused the earth to swallow up; and some We drowned; Allah did not wrong them; rather they wronged themselves."* (29:40)

Say: "Travel about the earth…"

Look at past peoples and the Prophets they were so hostile to, see what Allah did to them. See what happened to the peoples of Nuh and Salih and Hud and of Sayyidina Shu'ayb. In every single case of these peoples of the past those who followed their Prophets were saved and those who opposed their Prophets were all destroyed by Allah.

Say: "To whom does everything in the heavens and earth belong?" Say: "To Allah."

Everything in existence is an obedient slave to Allah. *"There is no one in the heavens and earth who will not come to the All Merciful as a slave."* (19:94) Not angels, not Prophets, not Messengers, they are all slaves of who, of *Sidi Mawlana.* All of them are subjugated to his Greatness and Majesty. And the people most fearful of Allah are the Prophets. As he said ﷺ, "I am the one of you who knows Allah best and the one who has the most fear of Him." Because the amount of knowledge a person has is measured by the amount of fear they have of Allah.

If you really know about Allah that: *"He knows the eyes deceit and what the breasts conceal."* (40:19) and that: *"We created man and We know what his own self whispers to him. We are nearer to him than his jugular vein."* (50:16) and *"He is with you wherever you are."* (57:4) If someone truly realises these things, realises that Allah is with them and watching them and looking at them, how can they disobey Him? People only disobey when they are unaware. For that reason unawareness is the greatest act of disobedience. But if a person is truly aware that Allah is watching them and seeing everything they do, they are bound to be afraid, and bound to pull back if they are about to do something wrong. They will say. "*Sidi Rabbi* I turn back to You."

There is a story about one of the people of Allah. He had a student who wanted to go and visit his family. He said, "Sidi, please give me some advice, a piece of counsel to take with me." He replied, "If you feel like disobeying your Lord, do it in a place where He can't see you. If you're going to do something wrong do it somewhere where *Sidi Rabbi* can't see you." So he left. Then when the idea of doing a wrong action occurred to him he said to himself, "*Sidi Rabbi* is watching me." Anyway his shaykh dissuaded him from committing wrong action in that way. "If you want to commit a wrong action, do it in a place where Allah can't see you." But nothing escapes Allah's sight: *"He knows the eyes deceit and what the breasts conceal."* (40:19) *"We created man and We know what his own self whispers to him. We are nearer to him than his jugular vein."* (50:16) That artery which if severed will cause a person to die.

He has made mercy incumbent on Himself.

That is something which we all live surrounded by all the time. *"He has made mercy incumbent on Himself."* By His bounty and generosity. No one can force Allah to do anything but He, *subhanah*, has made mercy mandatory on Himself. He sees the wrongdoer acting wrongly and yet He continues providing for him and He may even increase his wealth. He could in a second cause the earth to swallow him up or send down a thunderbolt on him, but instead He pardons him and excuses him in spite of his misdeeds and his turning away from Allah. How can that happen? It is because of the mercy that Allah imposes on Himself. *"He has made mercy incumbent on Himself."*

He will gather you to the Day of Rising about which there is no doubt.

All of us will be there on the Day of Rising but everything depends on what we have prepared for it. Everyone will be in a panic that Day, not knowing what Allah is going to do with them. People must think about the Next World, reflect on it and on what is going to happen to them on the Last Day, and the terrible hardships they will suffer on it. The sun comes right down over our heads, and our blood will start to boil; but if someone gives *sadaqa*, does good actions, that *sadaqa* will come and act as a shade for them; and those people who love one another for the sake of Allah and gather to do *dhikrullah* out of their love of Allah, they will be shielded from those hardships. They will be under the shade of the Throne "on the Day that there will be no shade except His shade." May Allah put us among those people by His bounty and generosity and give us love for one another in Allah and take us and you by the hand and take us and you on the path of success in this world and the Next.

10

al-An'am 6:13-18

وَلَهُۥ مَا سَكَنَ فِى ٱلَّيۡلِ وَٱلنَّهَارِ وَهُوَ ٱلسَّمِيعُ ٱلۡعَلِيمُ ۞ قُلۡ أَغَيۡرَ ٱللَّهِ أَتَّخِذُ
وَلِيًّا فَاطِرِ ٱلسَّمَٰوَٰتِ وَٱلۡأَرۡضِ وَهُوَ يُطۡعِمُ وَلَا يُطۡعَمُ قُلۡ إِنِّىٓ أُمِرۡتُ
أَنۡ أَكُونَ أَوَّلَ مَنۡ أَسۡلَمَ وَلَا تَكُونَنَّ مِنَ ٱلۡمُشۡرِكِينَ ۞ قُلۡ إِنِّىٓ أَخَافُ إِنۡ
عَصَيۡتُ رَبِّى عَذَابَ يَوۡمٍ عَظِيمٍ ۞ مَّن يُصۡرَفۡ عَنۡهُ يَوۡمَئِذٍ فَقَدۡ
رَحِمَهُۥ وَذَٰلِكَ ٱلۡفَوۡزُ ٱلۡمُبِينُ ۞ وَإِن يَمۡسَسۡكَ ٱللَّهُ بِضُرٍّ فَلَا كَاشِفَ لَهُۥٓ
إِلَّا هُوَ وَإِن يَمۡسَسۡكَ بِخَيۡرٍ فَهُوَ عَلَىٰ كُلِّ شَىۡءٍ قَدِيرٌ ۞ وَهُوَ
ٱلۡقَاهِرُ فَوۡقَ عِبَادِهِۦ وَهُوَ ٱلۡحَكِيمُ ٱلۡخَبِيرُ ۞

All that inhabits the night and day belongs to Him. He is the All-Hearing, the All-Knowing. Say: "Am I to take anyone other than Allah as my protector, the Bringer into Being of the heavens and earth, He Who feeds and is not fed?" Say: "I am commanded to be the first of the Muslims," And, "Do not be among the idolaters." Say: "I fear, were I to disobey my Lord, the punishment of a dreadful Day." Anyone from whom punishment is averted on that Day has been shown great mercy by Allah. That is the Clear Victory. If Allah touches you with harm, none can remove it but Him. If He touches you with good, He has power over all things. He is the Absolute Master over His slaves. He is the All-Wise, the All-Aware. (6:14-18)

Allah *'azza wa jall* says in His Mighty Book: *"All that inhabits the night and day belongs to Him. He is the All-Hearing, the All-Knowing."* We mentioned before that this *surah* is called *Surat al-An'am* and was sent down to the Prophet ﷺ at night accompanied by 70,000 angels. And the Prophet ﷺ was delighted to receive it. Allah *ta'ala* says in it: *All that inhabits the night and day belongs to Him.* *"Him"* here refers to Allah. Ibn Malik says that some words can simultaneously hold opposite meanings and the word *"sakana"* (*inhabits*) here is one of those. It means both what is still and also what moves about. So everything that is static in creation and everything that moves about comes from who? From Allah, may He be exalted. Everything thing in existence is brought about by Power, defined by Will, encompassed by Knowledge, and perfected by Wisdom. Everything in creation. Everything that is static, such as the mountains and the earth; they are static; and then we have things that move like the stars and sun and moon and people and animals; they all move and they are all slaves of Allah; and likewise everything that is static is also the slave of Allah. *"There is no one in the heavens and earth who will not come to the All Merciful as a slave."* (19:94) Everything is a slave to Allah. Whether unbeliever or Jew or Muslim everyone is a slave. Everyone is under the total control of our Lord and *"He misguides anyone He wills and guides anyone He wills."* (16:93) That is what is meant by His words: *All that inhabits the night and day belongs to Him.*

Then we have the phrase: *"He is the All-Hearing, the All-Knowing."* The All-Hearing is one of Allah's names and the All-Knowing is one of Allah's names. Allah has ninety-nine names and among them are the names All-Hearing and All-Knowing. The name All-Hearing is derived from the verb to hear and hearing is an attribute of Allah *subhanah*, a pre-eternal attribute. Allah has hearing by which He hears everything in the world, what is above it and underneath it. Nothing in existence escapes His hearing. So hearing is a pre-eternal Divine attribute. It connects with everything which is possible and necessary but is not connected to the impossible. He is All-Hearing, the One who hears the desires in our hearts and what occurs to them. Nothing in creation escapes His hearing. Neither in its heights nor its depths. Knowledge is also a Divine attribute, an attribute which covers everything, what is necessary, what is possible and also, in its case, what is impossible. So He, may He be exalted knows the world in its totality. He knows what attributes He has. And He knows that He has no associate and no equal. *"He is the All-Hearing, the All-Knowing."*

Say: "Am I to take anyone other than Allah as my protector..."

The reason for the revelation of this *ayah* is that when the Prophet ﷺ started to call people to Islam openly and paid no attention to anything the idolaters said to discourage him, the unbelieving idolaters wanted to devise some scheme to stop him and so they went to Abu Talib and said to him, "This nephew of yours, if it is power he wants, we will make him our king and we will also give him any women or wealth he wants; just so long as he does not say anything more against our idols." Abu Talib was the uncle of the Prophet but only Allah knows his state after he died. Abu Talib sat with him and said, "My nephew, listen to what these people are saying, they want to make you their leader and give you wealth and children, anything else you want, just so long as you give up calling people to Islam." In reply he said his famous words 🕮: "By Allah if you placed the sun and the moon..." and so on, "I will never give up this thing, until Allah decides the affair or we return to Allah."

There is no doubt that Allah did promise him success. Allah says: *"But Allah will perfect His Light, though the unbelievers hate it."* (61:8) From that time on they did their best to stop him; they didn't hold back; they didn't hold back from torturing him, from opposing him in every way they could. But the Prophet 🕮 was steadfast until Allah gave him victory over them. Allah says: *"Say: 'Am I to take anyone other than Allah as my protector...* " He told them, "No matter how much you try to bribe me, I will never take any protector apart from Allah." *Say: "Am I to take anyone other than Allah as my protector, the Bringer into Being of the heavens and earth,* "Do you expect me to leave the Creator of the heavens and the Creator of the earth to follow your idols, these false gods that can't bring benefit or harm. I am not stupid!"

"...the Bringer into Being of the heavens and earth..."

What is the meaning of "Bringer into Being"? It means Creator, Creator of the heavens and the earth. How can you equate Him with something that doesn't have any power to bring benefit or cause harm? They were stupid, they were worshipping idols and statues. It is true, of course, that they found their ancestors doing that and were following their example. But they couldn't say that thing about their forefathers when they knew the truth. It's not that they didn't know that the Prophet 🕮 was telling the truth. They did know. They used to call him, "the Trustworthy"; but once he came out with the Message they denied him. He didn't gain victory until after he had emigrated to Madina. That has all come from His words: *"Say: "Am I to take anyone other than Allah as my protector, the Bringer into Being of the heavens and earth,* "I am not going to leave the Creator of the heavens and earth, the One who has blessed me with all these different kinds of blessing, to follow your idols and statues. That's an impossibility, it's just not possible."

"...He Who feeds and is not fed?"

This is one of the attributes of the Truth, may He be exalted. The meaning of "feed" is provide for. Allah is the Provider. He feeds the whole world with His provision. Each creature is allotted its provision. There is no human being or animal or inanimate thing which is not given its provision by Allah. Allah, may He be exalted, is the Provider. He tells us: *"There is no creature on the earth which is not dependent upon Allah for its provision."* (11:6) Allah being the Provider encompasses everything, it is all inclusive. Allah provides the whole world with everything it needs. Everything receives the provision appropriate for it. This is from His words: *"He Who feeds and is not fed?"* Because He is the Rich beyond need, He does not eat or drink or sleep. He is independent of all things. In spite of this, there is one sound tradition in which He said, "I was hungry and you did not feed Me." He was asked, "How can You be hungry when You are the Lord of the worlds." He replied, "Did you not know that my slave, so and so, was hungry. If you had fed him you would have found Me with him." But, of course, the truth is that Allah *ta'ala* has no need of food or drink.

Say: "I am commanded to be the first of the Muslims,"

The Prophet ﷺ is told to tell us, "This thing I am guiding you to,

I am not telling you to do it when I'm not going to do it myself." No, the Prophet ﷺ used to stay up at night in prayer and used to go hungry and put up with persecution. He didn't tell people to be Muslims and not take it on himself. He was the first to take on Islam and was steadfast in the face of all the abuse the unbelievers hurled at him. Until Allah realised all his hopes, until Islam became generally accepted. *"But Allah refuses to do other than perfect His Light, even though the unbelievers detest it."* (9:32)

"And do not be among the idolaters."

The angel told him to tell them this; it wasn't an instruction to him; because idolatry in the case of the Prophet ﷺ is an impossibility. Because as far as idolatry is concerned, Allah addressed him saying: *"It has been revealed to me and those before me: 'If you associate others with Allah, your actions will come to nothing, and you will be among the losers.'"* (38:62) But Allah can address his slave as He wishes even though wrong action on the part of the Prophet is impossible. He was immune ﷺ from wrong action both before Prophethood and after it. No wrong action came from him, not intentionally, or by mistake, or unintentionally.

Say: "I fear, were I to disobey my Lord, the punishment of a dreadful Day."

This is a threat to us. If you disobey Allah, when do you get your come-uppance? On a dreadful Day. If someone disobeys Allah, He doesn't give them what's due to them straightaway because the door of repentance is always open as He tells us: *"But if anyone turns back to Allah after his wrongdoing and puts things right, Allah will turn towards him."* (5:39) and: *"...except for those who repent and believe and act rightly: Allah will transform the wrong actions of such people into good..."* (25:70) If a person weeps and fears Allah and implores Him for forgiveness and returns to the right path, it may well be that Allah will even turn what he's done wrong into a good action: *Allah will transform the wrong actions of such people into good –"* (25:70) Our Lord's door of forgiveness is wide open.

Anyone from whom punishment is averted on that Day has been shown great mercy by Allah.

You should know that the punishment of the Next World is very harsh, extremely severe. It's not like the fire we know in this world. It is seventy times as hot. If it was mild like that, it wouldn't be so bad but it is multiplied seventy times. If Allah averts the punishment from His slave, he has certainly been shown great mercy. But those who go to the punishment are in a terrible situation.

That is the Clear Victory.

That deflection of the punishment from you, that is the "Clear Victory".

If Allah touches you with harm, none can remove it but Him

This goes back to *tawhid*. *"If Allah touches you with harm, none can remove it but Him."* If someone becomes ill, for example, and looks for some means of relieving their illness, those means are all provided by who? By our Lord *ta'ala*. Those medicines and the doctor and everything he does, all of that, the person must recognize that it is Allah who has made it available to him. He mustn't, for instance, think that it is the doctor or the medicine which has made him better. That would be *shirk*. Because no means to a thing has any intrinsic effectiveness, no medicine, no doctor, or anything else for that matter. Our Lord, He is the doer in every instance. He is the one can do whatever He likes with His slave. And all these means that are used, the effect they have comes along with them not through them. When we eat we shouldn't think it is the food which makes us full, and when we drink we shouldn't say it is the water which quenches our thirst, and when we wear clothes we shouldn't think it the clothes which keep us warm, and so on, because means have no effect in themselves, the only effecter is Allah. Things come into being alongside their means not by them. "The means always exist but their redundancy must be recognised."

If He touches you with good, He has power over all things.

If Allah gives you something good, it is from the door of His bounty, of His blessing, even if it appears at the hands of a creature. An *ayah* in *Surat al-Jathiyya* tells us: *"And He has made everything in the heavens and earth subservient to you. It is all from Him.* (45:13) If someone attributes effectiveness to the means he is a *mushrik*, but his *shirk* is hidden not open. "So and so has given me, so and so supports me, or so and so did this thing for me." No, he must recognise that Allah is the Doer in every instance. But regarding the person who was the means, we must thank them, the means must be thanked. As the saying goes: "If someone is the means to a good thing for you, thank him for it," if someone helps you with something don't ignore him, either give him something or make *du'a* for him, but at the same time recognise that Allah is the Doer and the one who has subjected him to you. As for the other person he has, in reality, no power to do you either good or harm. Our Lord is the one who subjects him to you. As the *ayah* says: *"And He has made everything in the heavens and earth subservient to you. It is all from Him.* (45:12)

This is where most people go wrong; they forget and become heedless. They say, "This food is really good, it fills us up nicely," or "This water is lovely and cold, it really quenches our thirst," this is a mistake, this linkage. If the person saying that doesn't really believe it to be the effective cause, it's harmless, because Allah has made water the means to quenching the thirst, and made food the means to satisfying the appetite. But you must understand that that is not the thing itself which satisfies your appetite or quenches your thirst, because Allah is the one who creates the quenching in you and creates the satisfaction of your hunger. He tells us in *Surat as-Saffat*: *"Allah has created both you and what you do."* (37:96) All of it is the creation of our Lord.

He has power over all things. He is the Absolute Master over His slaves.

Glory be to Allah, there is no god but Him. *"Absolute Master"* al-Qahir is one of the names of Allah. Everything is subjugated by that name, it doesn't matter whether they are angels, or Prophets, or Messengers, or human beings or jinn, all of them are subjugated under the majesty of His Lordship. *"He is the Absolute Master over His slaves."* This being "over" things is metaphoric because our Lord is not restricted by aboveness or belowness, *"He is with you wherever you are,"* (57:4). We shouldn't say about the Throne, for instance, that it is far away from us. He said "No, I am with you wherever you are." And with the Throne Allah is making a metaphor of things connected with kingship, because every king has a throne, although, of course, Allah *ta'ala* is not in need of any throne.

He says: *"The All-Merciful, established firmly on the Throne,"* (20:4) He settled on the Throne with His All-Mercifulness and then the Throne disappeared into His All-Mercifulness, in the same way that all existent things disappear into the Throne. Our Lord, glory be to Him, has no need of anything. This Throne is nothing in the face of His overwhelming Power, but He has put it in place out of His Wisdom so that His Magnificence can be witnessed, the incomparable Magnificence of our Lord. Because this Throne has dimensions. There is a story of an angel who asked to reach its height and it flew for 30,000 years and didn't get anywhere at all, it couldn't do it; and then Allah gave more power to its wings and it still couldn't get anywhere, and why is that? This shows its unparalleled vastness, the indescribable vastness of the Throne.

He is the All-Wise, the All-Aware.

"The All-Wise" *al-Hakim*, in other words the one who puts things in their right place. If you want to know what wisdom is you need look no further than your own body. Allah tells us: *"And in yourselves as well; do you not then see?"* (51:21) Look at your hands, how they work, with their fingers and nails, and look at your face with its eyes and nose and two lips and teeth, and the ears you hear with: *"And in yourselves as well; do you not then see?"* (51:21) Look at the wisdom of our Lord manifested in your own body. However, we are not truly aware of ourselves. If we want to know Allah where must we look? We need look no further than our own bodies, which are nearer to us than anything else. Our Lord, glory be to Him is the Creator, the one who puts everything in its right place.

The All-Aware.

The one who discerns the intricate details of all things. The most minute particles which are completely invisible, He discerns all of them. *"Allah, Him from whom nothings is hidden either on earth or in heaven."* (3:5)

Say: "What thing is greater as a witness?" Say: "Allah."

Let's leave it there today. May Allah take us and you by the hand. And make us among those who love another in Allah. And seal our and your lives with happiness, with the seal which he grants His friends. And may He make our best and happiest day the day we meet Him.

11

al-An'am 6:18-20

وَهُوَ ٱلْقَاهِرُ فَوْقَ عِبَادِهِۦ وَهُوَ ٱلْحَكِيمُ ٱلْخَبِيرُ ۝ قُلْ أَىُّ شَىْءٍ
أَكْبَرُ شَهَٰدَةً قُلِ ٱللَّهُ شَهِيدٌۢ بَيْنِى وَبَيْنَكُمْ وَأُوحِىَ إِلَىَّ هَٰذَا ٱلْقُرْءَانُ لِأُنذِرَكُم
بِهِۦ وَمَنۢ بَلَغَ أَئِنَّكُمْ لَتَشْهَدُونَ أَنَّ مَعَ ٱللَّهِ ءَالِهَةً أُخْرَىٰ قُل لَّآ أَشْهَدُ قُلْ إِنَّمَا
هُوَ إِلَٰهٌ وَٰحِدٌ وَإِنَّنِى بَرِىٓءٌۭ مِّمَّا تُشْرِكُونَ ۝ ٱلَّذِينَ ءَاتَيْنَٰهُمُ ٱلْكِتَٰبَ يَعْرِفُونَهُۥ كَمَا
يَعْرِفُونَ أَبْنَآءَهُمُ ٱلَّذِينَ خَسِرُوٓا۟ أَنفُسَهُمْ فَهُمْ لَا يُؤْمِنُونَ ۝

*He is the Absolute Master over His slaves. He is the All-Wise,
the All-Aware. Say: 'What thing is greatest as a witness?' Say:
'Allah. He is Witness between me and you. This Qur'an has
been revealed to me so that I may warn you by it, and anyone
else it reaches. Do you then bear witness that there are other
gods with Allah?' Say: 'I do not bear witness.' Say: 'He is only
One God, and I am free of all you associate with Him.' Those
We have given the Book recognise it as they recognise their own
children. As for those who have lost their own selves, they have
no iman. (6:18-20)*

Allah *azza wa jall* says in His Mighty Book: "*He is the Absolute
Master over His slaves and He is the All-wise, the All-aware.*" We
have already told you that this *surah* is called *Suratu'l-An'am*

because Allah *ta'ala* mentions cattle in it. And it has 160 ayats. It came down to the Prophet in *Makkata'l-Musharrafa* except for a few *ayahs* which came down in *al-Madina*. We reached the place where Allah *ta'ala says*: *He is the Absolute Master over His slaves.* He is *al-Qahhir* – the Absolute Master. This is one of Allah's Names. *Al-Qahhir.* He is *Qahhir* over the oceans, all-powerful over them. He is the Absolute Master over the winds, All-Powerful over them. He is the Absolute Master over illness and health, they are completely under His power. He is the Absolute Master over His slaves. This being over them, when applied to Allah, is a matter of nobility and might. It is not matter of physical direction. We cannot refer to Him as being in any direction for, as He tells us: *"He is with you wherever you are."* (57:4) And also: *"Three men cannot confer together secretly without Him being the fourth of them, or five without Him being the sixth of them, or fewer than that or more without Him being with them wherever they are."* (58:7) So we can't say he is physically above the throne or above the heavens because only He truly knows how He is.

He is the All-Wise, the All-Aware.

The All-Wise – *al-Hakim* – is the one who puts everything in its right place. If you contemplate your own self you will know that He is *al-Hakim*. He puts the eyes in their right place and the nose in its right place and the same goes for the ears and the lips and the tongue. As He tells us in *Surat an-Naml*: that is all *"the handiwork of Allah…"* (27:88) All that is from His Name *al-Hakim*. *Al-Hakim* the one who puts everything in the right place. You don't have to look any further than your own body. Allah says: *"And in yourselves as well. Do you not then see?"* (51:21) He is *al-Hakim* and He is also *al-Khabir* – the All-Aware. He is the one who knows all the secrets of His slaves. He says: *"Allah – Him from whom nothing is hidden either on earth or in heaven."* (3:5) If a person realises that Allah really is All-Aware of him and has full access his innermost secrets and thoughts, he will certainly start to have fear of Allah. As He says: *"...fear Me if you are believers"* (3:175) because I am totally aware of what you do and watching you at every moment.

What thing is greatest as a witness? Say "Allah."

Those *mushrikun*, those idolaters of the people of Makka, they said, "We don't know anything about any Message. What we need is for the Jews and Christians, who have Books, we need them to witness that you are a Messenger. We have no idea what this Messengership business is about." So then they asked the Jews and they didn't confirm it and they asked the Christians and they didn't confirm it. This is the idolaters of Makka we're talking about. They said, "We asked the Jews, who know about that kind of thing, and they said, 'We don't have any information about any Messenger coming,' and we asked the Christians and they said they didn't know anything about any Messenger either." Then he said ﷺ, "I've got someone who will bear witness for me and that is *Sidi Mawlana, subhanah*, Himself. The best Witness for me is the One who sent down this Book to me, when, as you know, I had no formal education and cannot read or write. This testimony is far greater than any that the Jews and Christians could give you."

And the refusal of the Jews and Christians to bear witness was a lie in any case. They were lying because they actually knew perfectly well. Allah tells us: *"Those we have given the Book recognise it as they recognise their own sons. Yet a group of them,*" not all of them notice, "*a group of them knowingly conceal the truth.*" (2:146) Their saying that they didn't know about the Message – the Jews and Christians that is – was a lie. The scholars of the Jews knew and the scholars of the Christians, they knew too, because Allah mentions his description 🌸 and the description of his community in the Torah and gives his description and the description of his community in the Injil. It says in the Qur'an: "*Muhammad is the messenger of Allah*" and then mentions "*their likeness in the Torah,*" and their "*likeness in the Injil.*" (48:29) He described him 🌸 in the Torah and described him in the Injil as well. Their saying – that is the Christians – that they don't know that *Sayyidina* Muhammad is the Messenger of Allah – and the same goes for the Jews – is just a lie.

That all came from the great obduracy with which the idolaters of Makka insisted on holding to their *shirk*, because they were brought up worshipping idols and false gods. And their ancestors did the same. As Allah tells us: "*They said, We found our forefathers following a religion and we are just following in their footsteps.*" (43:22) They discovered their ancestors worshipping false gods and said they were just doing the same thing. The excuse they made was: "*We are only worshipping them because they bring us closer to Allah*" but that is a lie because you cannot get close to Allah except in the manner that He has ordained – except in the way He tells us – because our Lord has forbidden *shirk* and the worship of false gods and idols. Everything that that cuts you off from Allah, He has forbidden it.

He is Witness between me and you.

This witnessing of *Sidi Mawlana*, how does it take place? It is in His sending down to him of the Qur'an, in that bringing down to him by Jibreel, in every situation, of the *ayah* appropriate to it. The Qur'an is all the word of Allah. Where did Jibril bring it down from? From the presence of Allah Himself. Allah says: "*We sent it down on the Night of Power.*" (97:1) Allah sent it down on the Night of Power from the Preserved Tablet to the heaven of this world. Then He started sending it down in portions according to the situations that occurred. As He tells us: "*Every time they come to you with a difficult point, We bring you the truth and the best of explanations.*" (25:33) It came down first from where? From the *lawh al-mahfudh* – the Preserved Tablet – to the heaven of this world. Then Allah started sending it down in portions according to the situation, according to what was happening at the time. Anything that happened, Allah sent down the *ayah* that was appropriate to it.

This Qur'an has been revealed to me so that I may warn you by it, and anyone else it reaches.

This is the evidence. The Prophet ﷺ is saying: "The fact that I am unlettered, that I do not know how to read or write, is what bears witness to the truth of this Message. Allah has sent this Qur'an down to me and taught me the knowledges that are in it. Where could I have got all this knowledge from? How could I possibly have known these things by myself. The sending down of the Qur'an to me is in itself the proof of my Messengership, that I am a Messenger from Allah." At the moment we're talking about the Quraysh not the Jews and Christians. The Quraysh are the people referred to here. They denied the Messengership of the Prophet ﷺ saying, "We asked the Jews and they said they knew nothing about it and asked the Christians as well." As for information about the Jews and Christians themselves we'll get that in another *ayah* which is coming up soon.

This Qur'an has been revealed to me so that I may warn you by it, and anyone else it reaches.

In other words to make you fearful of Allah's punishment by it. Those idolaters knew nothing about Jahannam or the *Sirat* or the punishment of the Next World. They knew nothing about any of that. Then the Qur'an came and made it clear to them that Allah has created two abodes: an abode called Jahannam and the abode called the Garden. And made the matter of actions clear as well: those that take you to the Garden and others that take you to the Fire. The Qur'an makes it clear: *"As for him who overstepped the bounds and preferred the life of the dunya, the Blazing Fire will be his refuge. But as for him who feared the Station of his Lord and forbade the lower self its appetites, the Garden will be his refuge."* 79:37-40 Allah has made clear to us the path that leads to the Garden and the path that leads to the Fire. *But as for him who feared the Station of his Lord and forbade the lower self its appetites, the Garden will be his refuge."* And He says: *"The nafs indeed commands to evil acts – except for those my Lord has mercy on."*12:53 He makes the path clear to us and that is something that the Prophet ﷺ could never have known if he had not received these judgments and knowledges from Allah Himself. Because he was unlettered, he didn't know how to read or write and he never got together with any scholars or *ulama*. He only had what Jibreel came with and he was ordered to convey.

and anyone else it reaches.

That includes the People of the Book up until the Last Day. Whoever it reaches: in any country, in any direction. And anyone the Qur'an reaches, who doesn't believe in it, is judged to be an unbeliever. "...*so that I may warn you by it, and anyone else it reaches.*" This means that anyone the Qur'an reaches, whether that is in China or India or any other place, if the Qur'an reaches them and its meaning is understood, the judgment against them stands. Allah says: "*We never punish until We have sent a Messenger.*" 17:15 And what did the Messenger come with: the Qur'an. If people know of the Qur'an and become aware of what's in it, and don't believe in it, they come under the judgment of *kufr*.

so that I may warn you by it, and anyone else it reaches.

In other words "so that I may make you afraid by it." Allah induces fear before He mentions good news. Because the only thing that really turns the *nafs* back on its tracks is fear. Fear of Hellfire, fear of the *Sirat*, fear of the punishment of the Next World. If it feels fear it will turn back from the path of self-destruction. If it doesn't have any fear, it will just go on willy-nilly: "*The nafs indeed commands to evil acts – except for those my Lord has mercy on.*"

Do you testify that there are other gods besides Allah. Say I do not testify.

This is referring to when he, the Prophet ﷺ, said to the mushrikun, "You people say that there are other gods along with Allah." Those *mushrikun*, each one of them had his own idol, his own god. They asserted that they really were gods and they said, "*We only worship them to bring us closer to Allah.*" (39:3) But they had no evidence whatsoever for that. In any case they are unbelievers and, if they die in that state, they will be in the Fire forever.

Say: "I do not testify."

I do not testify that there is anything alongside Allah. Allah is one: "*Your god is one god.*" (37:4) They did not affirm the Divine Unity. They worshipped idols and false gods — to bring them closer, they said. But they had no evidence for that. It was just their own superstitions that made them think that. And this brings them under the judgment of *kufr* and means they will be forever in the Fire.

Say: "He is only One God."

Glory be to Him. Divinity is not subject to multiplication. As Allah tells us in *Surat al-Anbiya*: "*If there were other gods besides Allah in heaven or on earth they would both have been ruined.*" 21:22 If any other god existed the heavens and earth would never remain in place. But he is One God; it is He Who rules the whole universe. "*Glory be to Him who has the Dominion of all things in His Hand.*" (36:83)

"And I am free of what you associate."

This is the Prophet ﷺ talking. They invited him to agree with what they were doing but he refused to do that. They said, "You just have to go along with our idols and then we'll accept your kind of worship." He said "No! Absolutely not! I am never going to agree that there is any god along with Allah."

"And I am free of what you associate."

"These idols and false gods you have fabricated and that you worship besides Allah, I cannot agree with your worship of them." This was because condoning them in any way might possibly have led to affirming the validity of worshipping them. He said, "I do not condone your worship of them in any way."

Those We have given the Book recognise it as they recognise their own children. As for those who have lost their own selves, they have no iman.

Now we've reached the people of the Book. Those who were given the Book were the Jews and the Christians. *"Those We have given the Book recognise it as they recognise their own children."* That Abdallah b. Salam, when he became a Muslim, some of Companions met up with him in Madina. They asked him, "How did you come to recognise that the Prophet ﷺ was a Messenger?" He said, "I just saw him and noted his characteristics and I recognised him in the same way I know my own child." That was Abdallah b. Salam and he went on, "And not just me. Anyone who reads the Torah will know the Prophet as they know their own children." Those scholars and people of knowledge among the Jews knew about the Prophet; it was mandatory knowledge for them. But envy, and

I seek refuge with Allah from it, envy and desire for leadership prevented them from acknowledging him. They had authority over their people and they were afraid that if they affirmed him this might remove their power from them. Desire for leadership is one of the great human vices. Although in truth there are two kinds of desire for leadership. Desire for leadership in this world, which is wanting power for other than the sake of Allah. That kind is blameworthy. But there is also desire for leadership in the *deen*, which is when you want to be the leader of some people in order to teach the *deen* and what will bring them closer to Allah. That is praiseworthy desire for leadership.

As for those who have lost their own selves, they have no iman.

Every Jew and Christian has a place reserved for them in the Garden and a place reserved for them in the Fire. The Jews and Christians have a place in the Garden and a place in the Fire. And the same goes for the Muslims; they also have a place in the Garden and a place in the Fire. The difference is that the believers get a double reward: they enter their own place in the Garden and they also inherit the place of that Jew or Christian as well so they are rewarded twice over. If someone is a believer he enters his place in the Garden and inherits the place of a Jew or Christian as well. He has two places: one place through inheritance and one place by virtue of his actions. A place by actions and a place by inheritance. The Jew and Christian, on the other hand, get two punishments: they get the place of a Muslim in Jahannam as well as their own. So they combine two punishments, their own punishment and also the punishment of a Muslim, the Muslim's place in the Fire. That's a tremendous benefit for the believers.

They profit from their own actions and also inherit the possible good actions of either a Jew or Christian. One reward comes by inheritance and the other through their actions.

Who could do greater wrong than someone who invents lies against Allah.

Let's leave it there today. I'm doing as much with you as I possibly can.

12

al-An'am 6:21-26

وَمَنْ أَظْلَمُ مِمَّنِ افْتَرَىٰ عَلَى اللَّهِ كَذِبًا أَوْ كَذَّبَ بِآيَاتِهِ إِنَّهُ لَا يُفْلِحُ الظَّالِمُونَ ۝ وَيَوْمَ نَحْشُرُهُمْ جَمِيعًا ثُمَّ نَقُولُ لِلَّذِينَ أَشْرَكُوا أَيْنَ شُرَكَاؤُكُمُ الَّذِينَ كُنْتُمْ تَزْعُمُونَ ۝ ثُمَّ لَمْ تَكُنْ فِتْنَتُهُمْ إِلَّا أَنْ قَالُوا وَاللَّهِ رَبِّنَا مَا كُنَّا مُشْرِكِينَ ۝ انْظُرْ كَيْفَ كَذَبُوا عَلَىٰ أَنْفُسِهِمْ وَضَلَّ عَنْهُمْ مَا كَانُوا يَفْتَرُونَ ۝ وَمِنْهُمْ مَنْ يَسْتَمِعُ إِلَيْكَ وَجَعَلْنَا عَلَىٰ قُلُوبِهِمْ أَكِنَّةً أَنْ يَفْقَهُوهُ وَفِي آذَانِهِمْ وَقْرًا وَإِنْ يَرَوْا كُلَّ آيَةٍ لَا يُؤْمِنُوا بِهَا حَتَّىٰ إِذَا جَاؤُوكَ يُجَادِلُونَكَ يَقُولُ الَّذِينَ كَفَرُوا إِنْ هٰذَا إِلَّا أَسَاطِيرُ الْأَوَّلِينَ ۝ وَهُمْ يَنْهَوْنَ عَنْهُ وَيَنْأَوْنَ عَنْهُ وَإِنْ يُهْلِكُونَ إِلَّا أَنْفُسَهُمْ وَمَا يَشْعُرُونَ ۝

Who could do greater wrong than someone who invents lies against Allah or denies His Signs? The wrongdoers are certainly not successful. On the Day We gather them all together, We will say to those who associated others with Allah, 'Where are the partner-gods, for whom you made such claims?' Then they will have no recourse except to say, 'By Allah, our Lord, We were not idolaters.' See how they lie against themselves and how what they invented has forsaken them! Some of them listen to you but We have placed covers on their hearts, preventing them from understanding it, and heaviness in their ears. Though they were to see every sign, they still would not believe, so that when they come to you disputing with you, those who disbelieve say, 'This is nothing but the myths of previous peoples.' They keep others from it and avoid it themselves. They are only destroying themselves but they are not aware of it. (6:21-26)

Allah says in His mighty Book: *"Who could do greater wrong than someone who invents lies against Allah."* We have said before that this *surah* is called *Surat al-An'am* and that it contains 160 *ayahs* and came down to the Prophet ﷺ in Makka except for a few *ayahs*. In any case, this *surah* contains great benefits. In it there are commands, in it there are prohibitions and in it there are threats. A human being should only do those actions which have Allah's approval. We reached His Words: *"Who could do greater wrong..."*

Wrong or injustice is of two kinds: injustice with respect to creatures and injustice relating to what is between the slave and his Lord. It is the injustice between the slave and His Lord that we're going talk about today. As for the injustice with respect to creatures, a person has to protect himself from that sort of injustice, because Allah will not forgive him until the person he has wronged forgives him. That goes under the name of "the rights of the slave". If you know you have been unjust to somebody, go to that person and say, "I've wronged you or done something against you, forgive me for the sake of Allah." That will be sufficient for anything you have done. That is injustice with regard to creatures.

However, the injustice we are going to talk about now relates to what is between the slave and his Lord. What is the essential nature of this injustice on the part of the slave? It is for him to associate a partner with Allah. That is because our Lord, *subhanah*, has no partner and He has no child and no spouse and no equal. He, *subhanah*, is rich beyond any need of anything of that nature. Anyone who attributes to Allah anything not appropriate to Him has wronged Him and this kind of injustice is the greatest of all injustices. The implication of Allah's words: *"Who could do greater wrong than someone who lies about Allah..."* is that there is, in fact, no greater wrong that anyone could do than that, that that is the greatest act of injustice that it is possible for anyone to perpetrate. The *Jalalayn* says, corroborating this, that what is meant here is the attribution of a partner to Allah. But Our Lord, *subhanahu*, has no partner. As He says: *"There is no one in the heavens and earth who will not come to the All-Merciful as a slave."* 19:94 No angel, no Prophet, no Messenger: all of them are slaves to *Sidi Mawlana, subhanah*. *"There is no one in the heavens and earth who will not come to the All-Merciful as a slave."* 19:94 So this is talking about someone who attributes a partner to Allah, who commits *shirk*.

As we've said before there are two types *shirk*. One kind of *shirk* takes you out of the *deen*. That is when someone actually believes that Allah has a partner who can help him or harm him or give to him or withhold from him. Such a person, what about him? He's a *kafir*. No doubt about that. He's a *kafir*. Then there's also what's called hidden *shirk*. Hidden *shirk* is to attribute effects to their causes. Many, many people make that mistake and it comes from forgetfulness of Allah. But anyone who remembers Allah a great deal will certainly come to have a true grasp of *tawhid* in all his action and inaction.

If someone is forgetful of Allah they will say, for instance, that such and such a thing did them good. That is hidden *shirk*. They are forgetful of the fact that it is Allah alone who brings benefit.

Or they may say such and such a person harmed me, in which case they are forgetful of the fact that it is Allah alone who can do that. He alone is the Benefitter and He alone is the Harmer. Or you may say so and so gave me this thing. It is true that that person was the means for giving it to you. But who made them do it? No one but Our Lord, *subhanah*.

He Himself says concerning this: "*Most of them do not believe in Allah without associating others with Him.*" 12:106 And the Prophet ﷺ said, "*Shirk* in my community is more hidden than the track of an ant on a dark night on a hard rock." They said, "Messenger of Allah who can be safe from that, if it is so hidden that it cannot be seen?" But then he taught them a *dhikr* to protect themselves from it. He told them to say: "*Allahumma innee audhu bika an ushrika bika wa ana a'lam wa astaghfiruka lima la a'lam.*" "O Allah I seek refuge with You from associating something with You knowingly and I ask Your forgiveness for doing it unknowingly." If you want to do something with some people and to guard yourself from committing this kind of *shirk* in your dealings with them, then say: "*Allahumma innee audhu bika an ushrika bika wa ana a'lam wa astaghfiruka lima la a'lam.*" "O Allah I seek refuge with You from associating something with You, knowingly and I ask Your forgiveness for doing it unknowingly." Don't leave that place without saying: "*Allahumma innee audhu bika an ushrika bika wa ana a'lam wa astaghfiruka lima la a'lam.*" "O Allah I seek refuge with You from associating something with You, knowingly and I ask Your forgiveness for doing it unknowingly." That removes that hidden *shirk*: which is the attribution of things that happen to the means through which they come about.

The existence of means is an unavoidable fact of life. Our food, our drink, our clothes and other things, all these things are means. We see these things going together with what comes about. But what we must realise that in reality these means just accompany what happens, they are not the cause of it. It's a bad mistake to think that. These means, their existence is inevitable. When you get hungry you have to eat; but, at the same time, you have to realise that the satisfaction of your hunger is an act of Allah. You are bound to get thirsty and then you have to have something to drink; but the one who quenches your thirst is Allah. And you are bound to put on clothes to prevent yourself from getting cold; but you have to realise that it is Allah that makes you warm. And so on. The attribution of effects to causes is called hidden *shirk* and the only person safe from it is someone who remembers Allah a lot. Such a person knows that in reality Allah is the Doer of everything that happens. Allah says: *"Allah created both you and what you do."* (37:96) So Allah has created you but He also creates your actions.

or denies His Signs.

This is a reference to Allah's revealed Signs. There are two kinds of Signs: created Signs and revealed Signs. The created Signs are the fact that all created things in themselves testify to the Oneness of Allah. And we also have the revealed Signs which are the Qur'an and what has come down from the Prophet by way of hadiths. All those things are classified as *"Signs"*. Allah says about the action of the wrongdoers: *"or denies His Signs."* Their first denial is by attributing partners to Allah, and so denying the Divine Unity indicated by the created Signs. Their second denial is by denying the signs of the Qur'an. They said, "This is not a revealed Book, he is just telling you tales of the ancient peoples." These enemies of Allah wanted to mislead people, the ones who came to visit Makka. They were afraid the visitors would believe in what the Prophet ﷺ was reciting, because when he recited, it used to affect people's hearts. And when they were afraid of that happening, they would go to the leaders of the visiting groups and say to them, "Don't pay any attention to that, it's only tales of the ancient peoples."

Among the Makkans there was this man called Nadr, who knew all about the old kings, and he began to deceive them by saying, "Whatever stories he tells you, I can tell you better ones." But of course he was just lying and fabricating. Allah says about the Revelation: "*Nor does he speak from whim. It is nothing but Revelation revealed.*" (53:3-4) But that enemy of Allah, Nadr, he was eloquent and skilled in the use of language and he used to relate stories about past kings. He used to gather the people around him and address them saying, "I can tell you the same things he's telling you." And by doing that turned people away from Allah's *deen*.

The wrongdoers are certainly not successful.

The wronging that is being talked of here is injustice against creatures. If someone turns people away from the *ayahs* that came down to the Prophet ﷺ that isn't the kind of injustice we were talking about before, the kind that is between a person and Allah. Turning people away from the worship of Allah and acknowledgement of His Oneness is wronging them in the worst possible way. It is a huge injustice towards them. We already mentioned this wronging of other people. If someone hasn't done right by his wife or children, tomorrow on the Last Day Allah will ask him about that. I know some people here will have mistreated their wives. Tomorrow on the Day of Judgment they will be in an extremely ugly place.

As the hadith tells us: "All of you are shepherds and all of you are responsible for your flock." A man will be told: "This woman, *sidi*, you took her on and then failed to provide for her clothing and upkeep, and mistreated her." What's that going to lead to on the Last Day? It's going to put that man in a terrible situation. So if someone has done something like that, they should repent to Allah, turn back to *Sidi Rabbi*, return to treating Allah's slaves with kindness. The creatures of Allah that live with you, whether daughters or wives or children, you must be good to them. By Allah, if you do something against the things the *shari'a* says you should do, it will be terrible for you. If a woman is weak or poor and her husband leaves her hungry or sick or tells her to take care of her own affairs, that will result in a calamity between him and Allah. And on the Last Day he will be seriously questioned about it. I'm afraid there are many people here who do that, and they will have to answer for it.

On the Day We gather them all together

Tomorrow on the Day of Judgment everyone will be gathered together. Among them are people who committed *shirk*, who associated partners with Allah or attributed children to Him, like those who say, for instance, the angels are the daughters of Allah, or who say "Uzayr is the son of Allah" or say, "the Messiah is the son of Allah". All of that is attributing to Allah what is not appropriate for Him.

We will say to those who associated others with Allah, "Where are the partner-gods, for whom you made such claims?"

It is Our Lord who is addressing them here asking them the whereabouts of those gods of theirs they made partners with Allah. He continues:

Then they will have no recourse except to say, "By Allah, our Lord, We were not idolaters."

Then they are called to account, and they have to make some kind of reply, they know deep down that they have been worshipping idols and false gods; *fitna* here has the meaning mounting a defence, and the only defence they have is to say, "By Allah, our Lord" so they are making an oath when they do it, "We were not idolaters" They even make an oath denying it. But the truth is they are idolaters. But they swear that they were never idolaters. So they combine their lie with an oath.

See how they lie against themselves.

Lying is saying something which is other than what actually did happen. If somebody says something which didn't happen, he is called a liar. There are two kinds of lying: lying about Allah and lying about creation. One kind of lying is worse and uglier and that is lying against Allah.

See how they lie against themselves and how what they invented has forsaken them!

Because those idols and false gods – the ones they say they were worshipping – they disown them. Allah tells us: *"When those who were followed disown those who followed them,"* 2:165

Some of them listen to you but We have placed covers on their hearts, preventing them from understanding it,

Five enemies of the Prophet 🕊, among them Nadr, gathered round the Prophet and said to him, "Recite to us that Qur'an of yours." That Nadr we mentioned earlier he used to travel about and gather stories of the ancient peoples. King so and so did such and such; talking of the old kings, what they said. When the Prophet 🕊 stopped reciting, Nadr would say, "I can tell you better stories than that." He would relate to them, that Nadr, what happened with the old kings and governors and other such matters; and all this just to distance them from Islam and from *iman*. Then Allah says: "*but We have placed covers on their hearts...*" Allah has sealed up their hearts so they cannot see the true and only see the false.

and heaviness in their ears.

Allah removed the power of hearing from their ears so they couldn't hear the Qur'an in the way we hear it. Allah wanted them to be distanced and to be in misery, damnation and to be eternally in the Fire.

Though they were to see every Sign, they would still not believe

Even if they came back they would return to being how they were before. If they were sent back to the *dunya* they would be the same as they were before. That is because they were ordained to be like that. If someone is ordained to be an unbeliever, there is no way they can be anything but an unbeliever. If such a person comes back and says I'm going believe this time, he will just revert to his *kufr*.

so that when they come to you, disputing with you

This goes back to what we were talking about before, when they said, "This thing you're talking about, we know better stories than them." That Nadr who was so eloquent and used to address them.

those who are kafir say, "This is nothing but the myths of previous   peoples!"

He said this is just myths of the previous peoples. But what is he in fact referring to when he says that? He is referring to the stories the Prophet ﷺ received from Allah informing them about the people of Sayyidina Musa, and Sayyidina Isa and Sayyidina Nuh, and what happened to them. They were Allah's words. *Mawlana, subhanah*, was the one telling the stories. Allah says: "*We have given you all this news about the Messengers so We can make your heart firm by means of it.*" 11:119 These stories, *Mawlana, subhanah*, sent them down to the Prophet ﷺ to reassure him. When he was made aware of what happened between the people of Nuh and Sayyidina Nuh, and the people of Hud and Sayyidina Hud, the people Salih and Sayyidina Salih, it made it easier for him when he became discouraged, because all of them were injured, persecuted in the Way of Allah. There wasn't any Prophet or Messenger who wasn't harmed for the sake of Allah.

They keep others from it and avoid it themselves.

It is said that this *ayah* was sent down about the uncle of the Prophet ﷺ, Abu Talib. Abu Talib had a great deal of love for the Prophet ﷺ and used to defend him, but when he ﷺ asked him to believe, he couldn't do it. He didn't want to believe. There's a wisdom in this because, had he believed, he would have become the enemy of the idolaters and that would have made things much more difficult for the Prophet ﷺ. So there was a hidden benefit in his failure to believe. And there was disagreement after his death about whether he died as a believer or an unbeliever. There's controversy about it.

When he was close to death, the Prophet ﷺ came to him and found Abu Jahl and his cronies there with him. He said "Uncle, say that phrase which will enable me to testify for you in the presence of Allah, say *la ilaha illa'llah, Muhammadun rasulullah.*" But he was silent and didn't respond. Abu Jahl said to him "Watch out that you don't leave the belief of your ancestors; all of them worshipped idols and statues." And the Prophet ﷺ left without hearing the words of the *shahada.* But after he left Sayyidina al-Abbas went in. This is how it is said that in fact Abu Talib died a Muslim. Sayyidina al-Abbas went in and found him on the point of death. He said, "Brother, you really ought to follow your nephew. By Allah, he is on a true path." Abu Talib said, "Bear witness that I say that I witness that there is no god but Allah and that Muhammad is the Messenger of Allah." This is why there is this disagreement; because it didn't happen between him and the Prophet but Sayyidina al-Abbas used to affirm that he became Muslim in his presence. And that he said, *"La ilaha illa'llah, Muhammadun rasulullah."*

All right we'll leave it here today. We were saying a few things about Ramadan. The Prophet ﷺ said, "Whoever stays up in Ramadan out of *iman* in expectation of the reward, all his past wrong actions are forgiven." And it has come down: "Whoever stays up on the *laylatu'l-qadr* out of *iman* in expectation of the reward, all his past wrong actions are forgiven." And in another narration: "And his future wrong actions as well." All this is reminding us that people should take advantage of this month of Ramadan and do their best to perform as many good actions as they can. Because, as we have already told you several times, a *nafila* in Ramadan has the same reward as a *fard* at any other time. If you do a *nafila* you get the reward of a *fard*. And if you do a *fard* Allah gives you the reward of seventy *fards* outside Ramadan. So if someone misses out some things during the course of the year, they should make them up in Ramadan. If they strive to do good actions in Ramadan, Allah will forgive them for that.

"Whoever stays up in Ramadan out of *iman*..." in what Allah has promised, "in expectation of the reward..." doing it sincerely for the sake of Allah *ta'ala*, out of submission to the command of Allah. Allah has ordered him to fast and he fasts out of submission to Allah's command and believing in the reward Allah *ta'ala* has promised him. And if someone does fast because has been commanded to by Allah and believes in the reward He has promised us, what is the result? They are forgiven any past wrong actions they have done and it is also said both his past wrong actions and also any future ones. This is what has come down about Ramadan.

The same thing has also come down about *laylatu'l-qadr*. Allah says: "*Certainly We sent it down on the Night of Power...*" and: "*The Night of Power is better than a thousand months...*" Allah will give you a reward equivalent to that of a thousand months. That applies to whoever stays up for the *laylatu'l-qadr*. But what constitutes "staying up". Does it mean that you have to stay up after praying 'isha and carry on saying *Allahu akbar* until *fajr* arrives? Is that what is expected? The *ulama* say that if someone is weak they should, as a minimum, pray *salatu'l-isha* in *jama'a*, going by the hadith: "If someone prays *'isha* in *jama'a*, it is as if they had stayed up the whole night..." If you pray *'isha* with the *jama'a* and then do a couple of light *rakats*, it is "as if you had stayed up the whole night." There are other people who manage to stay up half the night. And there are those to whom Allah *tabaraka wa ta'ala* gives the strength to stay up the whole night. However, the truth is that if you realised the benefits and rewards which Allah gives for it, you would certainly take full advantage of it. Just take a little rest and then go back to your *'ibada*. May Allah give us and you success. And give us love for one another in Allah.

13

al-An'am 6:26-31

وَهُمْ يَنْهَوْنَ عَنْهُ وَيَنْأَوْنَ عَنْهُ وَإِن يُهْلِكُونَ إِلَّا أَنفُسَهُمْ وَمَا يَشْعُرُونَ ۝ وَلَوْ
تَرَىٰ إِذْ وُقِفُوا عَلَى ٱلنَّارِ فَقَالُوا يَٰلَيْتَنَا نُرَدُّ وَلَا نُكَذِّبَ بِـَٔايَٰتِ رَبِّنَا وَنَكُونَ
مِنَ ٱلْمُؤْمِنِينَ ۝ بَلْ بَدَا لَهُم مَّا كَانُوا يُخْفُونَ مِن قَبْلُ وَلَوْ رُدُّوا لَعَادُوا لِمَا نُهُوا
عَنْهُ وَإِنَّهُمْ لَكَٰذِبُونَ ۝ وَقَالُوٓا إِنْ هِيَ إِلَّا حَيَاتُنَا ٱلدُّنْيَا وَمَا نَحْنُ
بِمَبْعُوثِينَ ۝ وَلَوْ تَرَىٰ إِذْ وُقِفُوا عَلَىٰ رَبِّهِمْ قَالَ أَلَيْسَ هَٰذَا بِٱلْحَقِّ قَالُوا بَلَىٰ
وَرَبِّنَا قَالَ فَذُوقُوا ٱلْعَذَابَ بِمَا كُنتُمْ تَكْفُرُونَ ۝ قَدْ خَسِرَ ٱلَّذِينَ كَذَّبُوا بِلِقَآءِ ٱللَّهِ
حَتَّىٰ إِذَا جَآءَتْهُمُ ٱلسَّاعَةُ بَغْتَةً قَالُوا يَٰحَسْرَتَنَا عَلَىٰ مَا فَرَّطْنَا فِيهَا وَهُمْ يَحْمِلُونَ
أَوْزَارَهُمْ عَلَىٰ ظُهُورِهِمْ أَلَا سَآءَ مَا يَزِرُونَ ۝

*They keep others from it and avoid it themselves. They are
only destroying themselves but they are not aware of it. If only
you could see when they are standing before the Fire and saying,
'Oh, if only we could be sent back again, we would not deny the
Signs of our Lord and we would be among the believers.' No, it
is simply that what they were concealing before has been shown
to them; and if they were sent back they would merely return to
what they were forbidden to do. Truly they are liars. They say,
'There is nothing but this life and we will not be raised again.
If only you could see when they are standing before their Lord.*

He will say, 'Is this not the Truth?' They will say, 'Yes indeed, by our Lord!' He will say, 'Then taste the punishment for your unbelief.' Those who deny the meeting with Allah have lost, so that, when the Hour comes upon the suddenly, they will say, 'Alas for how we neglected it!' They will bear their burdens on their backs. How evil is what they bear! (6:26-31)

Allah *tabaraka wa ta'ala* says: "*They keep others from it and avoid it themselves. They are only destroying themselves but they are not aware of it.*" There is disagreement among the *mufassirun* about exactly what this *ayah* refers to. It is said that came down about the *mushrikeen*, because they used to run away from listening to the revelation that came to the Prophet ﷺ whenever they saw anyone approaching him they would threaten them to keep them far away from hearing the Prophet ﷺ; so they themselves did not benefit and they also stopped anyone else from benefitting. They themselves ran away from hearing the revelation that came down to the Prophet ﷺ and if they saw any other group trying to listen, they would threaten them so that they too would run away from hearing the revelation. So Allah says: "*They keep others from it and avoid it themselves.*" They keep others from what? From sitting with the Prophet ﷺ "*and avoid it themselves.*" In other words they also kept their distance from it; they ran away from it and made others run away; they fled and made other people flee away from it.

And what was the result of doing this: "*They are only destroying themselves*" On the Day of Judgment they will be taken to account both on their own account and also on account of everyone else they kept away from hearing the revelation of the Prophet ﷺ. So Allah will punish them twice. A punishment relating to their own running away from hearing the revelation from the Prophet ﷺ and also because if they found a group of poor and weak people who were listening to the Prophet ﷺ so that they could hear the revelation, they would threaten them until they drove them away from him. So as we said: *"They keep others from it and avoid it themselves but they are not aware."* They are responsible for the destruction of their own selves and also the destruction of anyone else they drove away from listening to the Revelation from the Prophet ﷺ.

If only you could see when they are standing before the Fire

We are all going to stand before the Fire not just them. *"If you could only see when they are standing before the Fire"*, when they actually see the Fire with their own eyes.

and saying, 'Oh! If only we could be sent back again

People who neglected the prayer will say, "If only we could go back and do the prayer"; anyone who neglected to pay *zakat* will say, "If only I could go back to the *dunya* and pay what I owed"; anyone who had some duty they didn't fulfil, which put them in danger of Jahannam, all of them will be afraid. People who fulfilled their obligations in the *dunya*, and spent their time worshipping Allah, and obeying Him and having *taqwa* of Him, they will escape. But anyone who fails to fulfil any of the obligations, or is able to go on Hajj and doesn't go, or has some dirhams and doesn't fulfil his obligation to pay the *zakat* owed on it, or is heedless of the prayer, or heedless of the fast, all such people will be afraid on the Day of Rising. They will say "Oh if only we could be sent back to the *dunya* to fulfil the obligations we missed."

But the time for that has passed because those obligations can only be fulfilled during our time in the *dunya*. This is the zone of action and the Next World is the zone of requital. The *dunya* is the zone of action and the Next World is the zone of requital. In the Next World there's no action, only requital. Allah tells us: "*Whoever does an atom's weight of good will see it. Whoever does an atom's weight of evil will see it.*" So as we said the *dunya* is the zone of action whereas the Next World is the zone of requital. So anyone who hasn't done the hajj will regret it; and anyone who has the ability to worship, or to stay up at night in prayer, or do *dhikr* of Allah, and then fails to do that, will regret it. Where? There where regret will be of no use to him.

and saying, "Oh! If only we could be sent back again, we would not deny the Signs of our Lord and we would be among the believers."

And does this do any good? No it is of no use at all! Why not? Because it is happening in the wrong place; because the place of action is the *dunya* and, as we said the Next World, is the zone of requital. If you do a good action you will get its due recompense where? In the Next World. And if you do a wrong action there is no doubt that you will receive full requital for it in the Next World. Anyway regarding that Allah says regret will be of no use to him there.

No, it is simply that what they were concealing before has been shown to them;

In other words the *kufr* they were concealing appears to them. Where will they see the requital for that *kufr* they were hiding? In the Next World. The *kufr* was in the *dunya* and the requital for that *kufr* takes place in the Next World.

and if they were sent back they would merely return to what they were forbidden to do.

They say "Please send us back to the *dunya*. We will believe, we will affirm the truth, and worship." But their misfortune will never be relieved because: *"if they were sent back they would merely return to what they were forbidden to do."* They would return to that *kufr* of theirs and to the wrong actions they used to do. Because those things were in any case written for them, so they would still be among the damned. If they were sent back the *dunya* they would just go back to the same state they were in before and then when they went back to the Next World they would see their punishment once again.

Truly they are liars.

They are liars when they say, "Our Lord send us back to the *dunya* and we will do good actions, rather than the ones we used to do." That's just a lie. No, if they were to return to the *dunya* they would simply return to the *kufr* and wrong actions they used to do before. Anyway whoever finds himself in a good state should praise Allah. So if someone is a believer and finds himself doing his prayers and worshipping Allah, he should know that Allah has manifested His bounty on him and been generous towards him. And if someone finds himself doing wrong, he too should know that that was written for him but he should not, for example, say, "O Lord you are the One who decreed for me to abandon the prayer, or decreed that wrong action." No, no, no! These things should not be said. Because Allah *ta'ala* has made the path to happiness abundantly clear to us and has also made the path to damnation clear to us. If a person wants to profit, they will take the path of happiness: its people are there, the knowledge is there, the Book and Sunna are in place. The case against anybody who commits *kufr* or wrong action is clear.

They say, 'There is nothing but this life and we will not be raised again.'

Now we come back to the people who completely deny the Resurrection. People who deny the Resurrection are *kafir*; there is no doubt about that. If someone says "I am a Muslim but I don't believe in the Next World," they are *kafir*. Because the Resurrection is something every human being must believe in. And not just the Resurrection either, the Resurrection and everything that goes along with it. If someone is eaten by a lion or drowned in an ocean, there is no doubt that they will still be brought back again in exactly the same form they had in the *dunya*. This is an absolute certainty. Allah will definitely bring them back to life again. Because as Allah says: *"His command when He desires a thing is just to say to it, 'Be!' and it is."* Allah *ta'ala* will return them to the original form they had in this world.

So when Allah says: *"They say, 'There is nothing but this life and we will not be raised again'"* those who say that are lying. The Resurrection will certainly take place and belief in it is essential – the Resurrection and what comes after it. We have the Resurrection and the person being returned to the original form they had during their lives in the *dunya*. And then there is also belief in the *Sirat*. Three thousand years it will take to cross it. A thousand going up it, a thousand going along it and then a further thousand going down the other side. Its slopes are steep and on each slope each person will be questioned about their *deen*, about how well they observed it. In one place they will be asked about their prayer, in another about *zakat*, in yet another about their fast; there will be a questioning place for every obligation. If they answer successfully they carry on, if don't they get held up there, some for ten years, some for a lot more than that. Anyway this is something most people are unaware of; they're fast asleep.

If only you could see when they are standing before their Lord.

Just now they were standing in front of the Fire, now they are standing in front of their Lord. Now it is their Lord who is examining them.

He will say, 'Is this not the Truth?'

It is the Truth *ta'ala* Himself who is speaking to them here, because they denied the Resurrection. They said "*There is nothing but this life and we will not be raised again.*" So when Allah has resurrected them and they have returned to the form they had in the *dunya*, the Truth *ta'ala* speaks them. He says to them, "What is this then? Is it not the truth?" And the Qur'an continues:

They will say: 'Yes indeed by our Lord.'

They have to admit that it is the truth. They can no longer deny it. At first, when they were standing in front of the Fire, they denied it. But now that the Truth has stood them in His Presence, He repeats to them the denial they made before. "*Is this not the truth?*" They admit it by saying: "*Yes indeed by our*

Lord." Now they admit the reality of the Resurrection. Then after that Allah says:

He will say, 'Then taste the punishment for your unbelief.'

He says: *'Then taste the punishment for your unbelief.'* Because they rejected the Prophet ﷺ and the Message he brought. They said, "We don't know anything about any Message." They rejected everything that the Messenger ﷺ brought, be it news of the Resurrection, or the *Sirat,* or the Garden or the Fire. Allah *ta'ala* will punish them for every single one of the pillars of belief they denied. All that will be decreed against them.

Those who deny the meeting with Allah have lost

The meeting with Allah can only take place by dying, only through death. *"Every self will taste death"* (3:185) *"Everyone on it will pass away..."* (55:26) *"All things are passing except His Face..."* (28:88) All of us are going to die. And after death all human beings will certainly be questioned. Questioned in their graves; questioned at their resurrection about their life; at every stage they will be questioned. This is a tremendous affair and yet people are fast asleep concerning it.

so that, when the Hour comes upon them suddenly,

Because it will only happen unexpectedly. During his life the Prophet ﷺ used to emphasise the closeness of this world to the Day of Resurrection. He said it was like two things very close together, like night and day. He said that if the time-span of this world is looked at as being the length of a day, then we have passed *dhuhr* and passed *asr* and all that is left of this world is sunset and

207

the sinking of the sun's disk below the horizon. He emphasised this closeness to instil fear into us. Anyone who really knows they are going to die is going to be very careful. They will realise that they have to make *tawba*, and that they only have a little time left to do it. Allah says: "*Turn to Allah every one of you, believers, so that you will be successful.*" (24:31)

Tawba is always possible and if someone has done a bad action, and does *tawba*, it's very possible that Allah may even turn their bad actions into good actions. If they say, for instance, in their *tawba* that they have committed wrong actions and have been heedless of Allah, but now they are turning back, returning to worship and obedience to Allah, and are going to keep company with the people of *dhikr* and good action. That is because you will inevitably be like whoever you keep company with. If someone is basically a good person but then keeps bad company, he will himself become bad. And in the same way if a bad person mixes with good people he will become good himself. Whoever you keep company with, you will become like them. I've known people who used to do *dhikrullah* and then, after a bit, left and went their own way; then their desires played havoc with them and the *dunya* and the *nafs* which commands to evil swept them away.

they will say, 'Alas for how we neglected it!' They will bear their burdens on their backs.

What an amazing thing! Those sins and wrong actions they did, Allah piles them onto their backs. Anyone who knows about all these things, how is it possible for them not to make *tawba* and return to Allah, *tabaraka wa ta'ala*. When someone knows they are going to be faced by the Next World, that they are going to face the Questioning, going to be questioned there about what they did, how can they not wake up. First there is the grave, then the Resurrection, then the *Sirat*; all the states of the Next World are in front of us, there to seen. If someone does not believe in these things they're fast asleep. And, of course, belief demands action. If someone believes in his heart, they're bound to act to profit from that belief. Belief on its own without action brings about loss, and what does loss mean, where will you go then, you will go to loss, you will go the Fire. Belief is only any use if it leads to profit not loss. Profit lies in striving for the Garden and loss is entering the Fire. The path that leads to the Garden is clear, as is the path that leads to the Fire. The path that leads to the Garden is right action. The path that leads to the Fire is wrong action and succumbing to the lower appetites.

How evil is what they bear!

All right, let's leave it there today. There's a little story told about Abdalwahhab ash-Sha'rani which I will tell you to get you ready to pay your *zakat al-fitr*. He fasted Ramadan and didn't have anything to pay his *zakat al-fitr* with. So there was his fast, suspended in mid-air, because that is what happens until your *zakat al-fitr* has been paid; nothing of what he had done was reaching Allah. He saw an angel and said to it, "My actions have not been accepted." The angel said, "The reason for that is that you haven't paid your *zakat al-fitr* yet." He said, "I'm a very poor man and I don't have anything to pay my *zakat al-fitr* with." The angel said to him, "I know you've got some little things stashed away in such and such a place. Go and get them and sell them and pay your *zakat al-fitr* with what you get for them!" So he did that and paid his *zakat al-fitr* and his Ramadan was accepted. So we should all remember that Allah keeps our Ramadan suspended between heaven and earth and it only rises up after our *zakat al-fitr* has been paid. May Allah give you and me success in doing right actions that are accepted by Him.

al-An'am 6:29-31

وَقَالُوٓاْ إِنْ هِيَ إِلَّا حَيَاتُنَا ٱلدُّنْيَا وَمَا نَحْنُ بِمَبْعُوثِينَ ۝ وَلَوْ تَرَىٰٓ إِذْ وُقِفُواْ عَلَىٰ
رَبِّهِمْ قَالَ أَلَيْسَ هَٰذَا بِٱلْحَقِّ قَالُواْ بَلَىٰ وَرَبِّنَا قَالَ فَذُوقُواْ ٱلْعَذَابَ بِمَا كُنتُمْ
تَكْفُرُونَ ۝ قَدْ خَسِرَ ٱلَّذِينَ كَذَّبُواْ بِلِقَآءِ ٱللَّهِ حَتَّىٰٓ إِذَا جَآءَتْهُمُ ٱلسَّاعَةُ بَغْتَةً
قَالُواْ يَٰحَسْرَتَنَا عَلَىٰ مَا فَرَّطْنَا فِيهَا وَهُمْ يَحْمِلُونَ أَوْزَارَهُمْ عَلَىٰ ظُهُورِهِمْ أَلَا
سَآءَ مَا يَزِرُونَ ۝

*They say, 'There is nothing but this life we will not be raised
again.' If only you could see when they are standing before their
Lord. He will say, 'Is this not the Truth?' They will say, 'Yes
indeed, by our Lord!' He will say, 'Then taste the punishment
for your kufr.' Those who deny the meeting with Allah have
lost, so that, when the Hour comes upon them suddenly, they
will say, 'Alas for how we neglected it!' They will bear their
burdens on their backs. How evil is what they bear! The life
of this world is nothing but a game and a diversion. The Next
World is better for those who have taqwa. So will you not use
your intellect? (6:29-32)*

Allah *ta'ala* says: They say, "*There is nothing but this life and we
will not be raised again.*" As we have said before this noble *surah*

is called *Surat al-An'am* and we have been looking at its meaning. We reached the *ayah* where Allah *ta'ala* says: *They say, "There is nothing but this life and we will not be raised again."* These idolaters of the people of Makka, enemies of Allah, at first they just denied the Qur'an. They said, "This is not the Word of Allah. We believe in you as a person but this thing you have brought us we don't believe in that." They then started to deny the Resurrection. *"They say, 'There is nothing but this life and we will not be raised again.'"* They said, "We only know this life, we don't know anything about this Resurrection business." Although the truth is that belief in the Resurrection is obligatory. If someone denies it, they are deemed to be a *kafir*. That is because it is mentioned in the Book and the Sunna and is the accepted consensus of the community.

After the human being has returned to dust, or been eaten by a fish, or drowned in the sea, there is no doubt that Allah will return them to the same state they were in this world. Allah says: *"It is He Who originated creation and then regenerates it. That is very easy for Him."* 30:27 He is the One who created you from a little drop of water and developed you in your mother's womb, turning you from drop to a clot to a lump of flesh to bones. So He was already nourishing you while you were in your mother's womb and then continued to nourish you when you came out after that and has done so throughout your whole life. So how can you be surprised at His bringing you back? He just has to say to something, "Be!" and it is. Our Lord: nothing is impossible for Him. There is nothing His Power, *subhanah*, is not able to do.

Belief in the Resurrection will certainly engender good action. Anyone whose belief in the Resurrection gets stronger, their good actions will definitely increase as well. And if their belief in the Resurrection gets weaker, their good actions will inevitably decrease. If someone truly realises they're going to die, and going to stand in front of Allah, and going to be held to account for every small and big thing they have done; if they really know that *"Whoever does and atom's weight of good will see it and whoever does an atom's weight of evil will see it."* In other words if they are certain they are going to be resurrected and given their account, in respect of their family, their relatives, their wealth and everything else they have to account for – knowing that they will either be safe on that Day or utterly destroyed – they will definitely do everything they can to succeed, in the sure knowledge that if they don't the consequences will be disastrous. If you are one of those who are successful, if you are someone who has fulfilled your obligations in the *dunya*, on the Day of Judgment you will be safe and be a winner.

But what about if you are someone who has not fulfilled the rights other people have over you? Where the rights of our Lord are concerned there's not so much of a problem, because our Lord is generous and merciful. It's the rights of other creatures that are the tough ones; that's where the problem lies. If you take something belonging to someone else and don't give it back to them before they die, or you try to do them down, or do anything else to harm them, these are all a matter of the rights other creatures have over you; they are distinct from the rights you owe to Allah. In that case your only hope is that that person, the one you owe the right to, excuses you. It is crucial for people to protect themselves from violating the rights of the other slaves of *Sidi Mawlana*. Allah loves His slaves and He doesn't like anyone who harms them or destroys them. You must be good to other people. As the saying goes: "Be good to other people just as Allah is good to you." If you are good to others and patient with them, you will find that that has good consequences but if someone is heedless of other people's rights, tomorrow on the Day of Judgment it will be very tough for him.

Allah says: "*They say, 'There is nothing but this life and we will not be raised again.'*" And elsewhere: "*It is He Who originated creation and then regenerates it. That is very easy for Him.*" 30:26. And again: "*His command when He desires a thing is just to say to it, 'Be!' and it is.*" 36:81 If a person really does have belief in the Resurrection, if he really knows, when he looks at his body, that it is going to be brought back to life, then he will be conscious of the fact that Allah is going ask him about it on the Day of Judgment. He will know that Allah is going to ask him about his sight and what he looked at, about his hearing and what he listened to, about his tongue and what he said with it, about his legs and where they took him to, about his hands and what he did with them, and about his heart and what was inside it; he will be asked about all these things on the Day of Judgment.

If they say good things about him, no harm will come to him, he will be all right; if there are problems, it becomes a matter of the Divine Will. If it is something Allah has ordained to be forgiven, the person will be saved, if not then it will result in his punishment. The root of all good actions is belief in the Resurrection and the accounting that comes with it. If anyone's belief in it weakens, their good actions will necessarily also decrease and if their belief in it strengthens their good actions will also increase. That's clear.

If only you could see when they are standing before their Lord.

In the earlier *ayah*, if you remember, they were standing in front of Fire. Now they are standing in front of their Lord – for the Reckoning. The angels will bring them tied up – those enemies of Allah the idolaters of the people of Makka and all those like them – they will be brought with their hands tied together to be given their account. Allah says: "*If only you could see when they are standing before their Lord.*" In other words their crimes will be addressed. If you could see them you would be amazed. When Allah has them standing in front of Him and says to them, "Why, when I sent you a Messenger guiding you to what would bring you close to Me, and to what would result in your entering the Garden, why did you then reject him and disbelieve in him, and associate other things with Me?" What will that result in? Their certain destruction.

"Is this not the truth?"

Allah asks them, "Wasn't it true then, that you would be brought back to life?" They answer:

"Yes indeed by our Lord."

Meaning that the Resurrection really is true. Before, when they were in this world, they did not accept it. They said, "We're never going to be resurrected. People just turn to dust and disappear." But now when they are asked: "*Is this not the truth?*" they answer: "*Yes indeed.*" What is the Resurrection? They were dust and then Allah says to them, "Revert to what you were like in the *dunya*." And they return to exactly the same form they had in the *dunya* and they're given their account.

He will say, "Then taste the punishment for your unbelief."

Why are they experiencing this? Because they rejected the Message of the Prophet 🌿 and the Qur'an he brought. They rejected the Message but they had complete faith in him 🌿 where their own affairs were concerned. They said, "From our experience of your behaviour with us we know that you are truthful. But as to all this stuff about a Message and the Qur'an, we don't believe in any of that." So they rejected what he brought. They had no faith in his Messengership and the Book of Allah. So Allah says: *"Then taste the punishment for your unbelief."* That unbelief of theirs lasts forever. *"They are in it timelessly forever."* Those who died idolaters, rejecting the Message and the Resurrection, denying all these things, those people are eternally in the Fire; there is no escape for them.

The wrong actions of the believers are not so disastrous. They are inevitably going to enter the Garden in the end. It is true that they will have to go through some sort of trial on account of what they did but the end result of their affair will be entrance into the Garden. Anyone who dies witnessing that there is no god but Allah and that Muhammad is His Messenger will enter the Garden. When the Prophet 🌿 said this he was asked, "Even if he fornicates and steals?" He 🌿 said: "Yes even if he fornicates and steals. Whether Abu Dharr likes it or not!" Do fornication and stealing not stop people entering the Garden? No because Allah covers them with His Forgiveness and His Mercy, because they are held up by the great supporting pillar, *la lilaha ill'llah Muhammadun Rasulullah.* Anyone who dies witnessing that there is no god but Allah and that Muhammad is the Messenger of Allah will enter the Garden regardless of the condition they are in. As long as there is no *kufr* or *shirk*, anything else is all right.

Those who deny the meeting with Allah have lost,

This does not, of course, just apply to those idolaters of Makka. Anyone who denies the Meeting with Allah and the Resurrection will inevitably be among the lost. "*Those who deny the meeting with Allah have lost.*" There is no doubt that all of us are going to stand before Allah and there is no doubt that all of us will see Him. The Prophet 🙵 was asked, "Will we see our Lord?" And he replied, "Is there any doubt about seeing the moon on the night when it is full!" He meant that of course that you can then see it clearly. And then he said, "That is how you will see your Lord." He will manifest Himself until we see Him and He will address us, speaking to each one individually.

so that, when the Hour comes upon them suddenly, they will say, "Alas for how we neglected it!" They will bear their burdens on their backs.

Those wrong actions they used to do will take on a tangible physical form. They will then go to the person who did them and say, "Show us your back so we can load ourselves onto it." So his burden is loaded onto him, that load of his wrong actions. They cease to be immaterial and become physicalised, solid bodies. For instance the lies someone told, or wine drinking they indulged in, or their disrespect to their parents, or any other major wrong actions they may have done, on the Day of Judgment all these things will take on a physical shape and climb onto the back of the one who did them.

How evil is what they bear!

What they are carrying on their backs. Because those wrong actions, they don't remain immaterial, they become physicalised, they become solid bodies to be carried by their perpetrator on his back.

The life of the *dunya* is nothing but a game and a diversion.

Allah tells us this in order to make us wary of this world, so we do not let it get into our hearts. You cannot do without this world. Our affairs can only be taken care of by means of the *dunya*. However the *dunya* is a double edged sword. Sometimes people gain from it and live by it but sometimes they let it get into their heart. They make it their prime objective; they let it distract them from the five prayers and from doing right actions; they make it their main occupation. The *dunya* becomes like a second wife for them and they do not allow any room for their other one. With two wives, if you please one too much, the other one will certainly suffer! If you give all your attention to the *dunya* you will not have anything left for the Next World.

A person must give everything its due. You have to take care of the affairs of this world but you must also do your five prayers, get up in the night a bit, ask forgiveness for your wrong actions, and not abuse other people's rights. Then you will be all right. But if you neglect these things on the Day of Judgment you will feel bitter regret when regret will be of no use to you whatsoever.

The Next World is better for those who have *taqwa*.

Wherever go you go you must have *taqwa*. A person can only

gain the Garden by having *taqwa*. There are different degrees of *taqwa*. The first level is protection from *shirk* and *kufr*. That's the first one. Next comes *taqwa* against major wrong actions, such as fornication and drinking alcohol and disrespect of one's parents and similar major wrong actions. Then against minor wrong actions. If someone refrains from all this they are called *mutaqqi* and, if they are *mutaqqi*, when they go on to the Next World they will go to the Garden and be free. So everyone must strive to have *taqwa*.

We have a great teacher in Imam al-Ghazali, who used to educate people in a very good and easy way. He said when someone gets up for *subh*, he should look at the day ahead of him and say to himself, "Today I am going to add another day to my life and I must make sure I do the five prayers on time and keep an eye on my limbs and senses so that they don't get involved in any wrong action." In any case he should talk to himself in this way and then keep a watchful eye on himself, on what happens to him during that day. At *dhuhr, 'asr, maghrib* and *'isha*. Then after *'isha* he should take himself to account, saying to himself, "How did I do today? I prayed *dhuhr* on time, *al-hamdu wa shukrulillah*." He should say to his *nafs* how did we do today? Some *dhikr, al-hamdu wa shukrulillah*. The same applies to *'asr, maghrib* and *'isha*." If this has been your day, you should do a hundred *hamdulillah wa shukrulillah* out of thanks to Allah for the success you have had from Him, thanks to the One who has enabled you to do it.

But if you have missed out on something, or some business came up and distracted you from the time of one of the prayers, whether that was *'asr* or *maghrib* or *'isha*, you should say to your *nafs*, "What have you done; you are making problems for me with *Sidi Rabbi*. On the Day of Judgment He's going to ask me about this time you wasted for me." And you should mete out a bit of punishment to it. For instance you could say, "Tomorrow I'm going to make you go hungry. You're not going to have any lunch tomorrow." The only way of training is the *nafs* is through hunger. You say, "You want to harm me but I am going to make you suffer first." If you make it suffer a little hunger and it will become obedient. It is only tamed by hunger. If you don't do that, what do think is going to happen? Tomorrow it will do something even worse.

So first you have *murabata* then *muraqaba* then *muhasaba* and lastly *mu'aqaba*: first the commitment to do right; then watchfulness to make sure you do it; then taking stock at the end of each day; then a bit of disciplining of yourself if you've slipped up. You have these four things by which you can bring your *nafs* to heel. First thing in the morning at *subh* you say to yourself, "Allah has been kind to me in adding another day to my life and I am under obligation to Him to do certain things: there are the rights other creatures have on me and the rights I owe to my Creator." You should keep a careful account of what you do. Then after *'isha* you should sit it down and say to yourself, "Now let's add up the account." As the saying goes: "Call yourself to account before you are taken to account. Weigh yourself before you are weighed." Put yourself in the scale here before you are put in the scale on the Day of Judgment. Call yourself to account in this world before you are called to account on the Last Day. "Call yourself to account before you are taken to account. Weigh yourself before you are weighed."

If you find yourself a winner you should do a hundred *hamdulillah wa shukrulillah*, to thank Allah for having given you success, because as we know from the *ayah* in *Sura Hud*: "*Wa ma tawfiqiya illa billah*" Our success is only by Allah. You know that it is *Mawlana* who has helped you, and given you success. He is the one who has enabled you to do those acts of obedience. If, on the other hand, you find yourself lacking, you should do some *istighfar*, asking forgiveness from Allah, because there is a hadith regarding this in which the Prophet ﷺ said, "Anyone who goes to bed and says: "*Astaghfirullah al-'adhim alladhi la ilaha illa hu al-hayyu al-qayyum wa atubu ilayh*" three times will be forgiven his wrong actions even if they are as much as the foam on the sea, or as many as the grains of sand on the shore, or as many as the days of this world, or all the leaves on all the trees." So remember this and when you go to bed do it. Say, "I ask forgiveness from Allah the Immense than whom there is no other god, the Living the All-Sustaining, and I turn to Him," three times, or if you want to do it ten or a hundred times do that.

The hadith specifies three times but if someone wants to do more they can. So that he will sleep purified of his wrong actions and he will start the day tomorrow clean, with a clean slate. But if someone goes to sleep with that dirt in his heart, without doing *istighfar*, then tomorrow again his heart will harden up. Allah *ta'ala* says in Qur'an: "*No indeed! What they have earned has rusted up their hearts.*" (83:14) That darkness will accumulate in his heart until the heart is so unclean and impure it will not incline to anything except to wrong action and lower appetites. This is why we have said that people should rectify themselves. First you should make a demand on yourself, then keep a close watch over it, then, at night, you should hold yourself to account and if you find you've done all right you should praise Allah but if you see something wrong you should ask forgiveness and discipline yourself for it.

The Next World is better for those who have *taqwa*. So will you not use your intellect?

We'll leave it that till tomorrow *insha'allah*. May Allah give us and you success in gaining good. And make us people who love one another in Allah. And seal us and you with happiness. And our king, may Allah help him to the good and give him close advisors who will help him to do good. And anyone who afflicts Allah's slaves, may Allah destroy them and give the Muslims victory over them, very soon, *insha'allah*. May Allah give us and you that state of happiness He has reserved for His *awliya* and make the best of our days the Day we meet Him.